1914: The Marne
& The Aisne

1914: The Marne & The Aisne

Two Accounts of the Early Battles
of the First Year of the First World War

The Battles of the Marne and Aisne

H. W. Carless Davis

Troyon an Engagement in
the Battle of the Aisne

A. Neville Hilditch

LEONAUR

1914: The Marne & The Aisne
Two Accounts of the Early Battles
of the First Year of the First World War
The Battles of the Marne and Aisne
by H. W. Carless Davis
and
Troyon an Engagement in the Battle of the Aisne
by A. Neville Hilditch

First published under the titles

The Battles of the Marne and Aisne
and
Troyon an Engagement in the Battle of the Aisne

Leonaur is an imprint of Oakpast Ltd

Copyright in this form © 2011 Oakpast Ltd

ISBN: 978-0-85706-541-4 (hardcover)
ISBN:978-0-85706-542-1 (softcover)

http://www.leonaur.com

Publisher's Notes

Contents

The Battles of the Marne and Aisne

H. W. Carless Davis

Contents

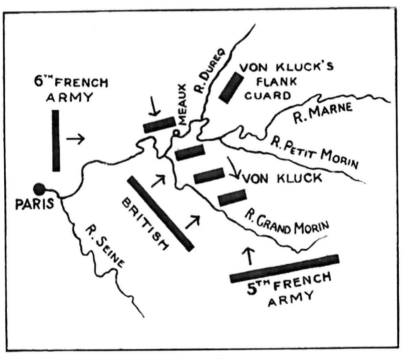

THE OPENING POSITION

Introduction

The documents which are printed in this book describe the operations of the British Expeditionary Force in France from August 28 to September 28. Nos. 1 and 2 are the official despatches of Field-Marshal Sir John French. Appendices A and B are also official. They were written by an officer attached to the General Headquarters' Staff and were published by the Press Bureau; they relate to operations on the Aisne from the 10th to the 17th of September inclusive. They are interim reports, often studiously vague as to details; but they give an admirable picture of the terrain and of the general features of the British operations. The second of them contains some remarkable extracts from the letter of a German soldier describing the operations of the German 10th Army Corps from the 6th to the 9th of September inclusive.

From August 27 to September 3 inclusive the British Force continued to take part in the general retrograde movement which had been ordered by General Joffre. But the pressure of the enemy on the British rear was less dangerous than it had been on the retreat from Mons to La Cateau. Sir John French makes it clear that, when once General Joffre had ascertained the scale and object of the German flanking movement, from which the British troops had suffered so severely, the left of the Allies' line was promptly extended and consolidated. Two French armies, the 7th and the 6th, were brought up to the neighbourhood of Amiens and of Roye, where they covered the British left.

On the 28th the British Force had reached the line of the

Oise and covered the line La Fère-Chauny-Noyon. The Germans were advancing upon the centre of this position, by way of Ham, in great strength. The pressure was relieved by a counter-attack of the 5th French Army, which held the line, to the right of the British Force, from La Fère to Guise; and under cover of this operation Sir John French retired on the 29th, towards the river Aisne, between Compiègne and Soissons. It is clear that the 7th and 6th French Armies on his left were also retiring fast; for at this point he thought it wise to abandon the line of communications through Amiens to Havre, and to remove his sea-base to the mouth of the Loire.

But the retirement was now deliberate and confident; as the retreating line of the Allies was lengthened, more and more French troops were thrust into the gaps and weak points. Both the British and the French fought rearguard actions with success; the British First Cavalry Brigade distinguished themselves particularly by a desperate counter-attack in the forest of Compiègne; but no attempt was made to follow up such advantages. On September 3 the British forces were south of the Marne, where they stretched like the string of a bow across the loop which the river makes between Lagny on the west and La Ferté on the east. On September 5, by the desire of General Joffre, they were still further to the south, behind the line of the Grand Morin, a tributary of the Marne.

The Germans were already crossing the Marne in strength; but from September 3 it had become evident that they were moving south-east on Montmirail. This operation left their right flank exposed to attack from the left wing of the Allies; and accordingly General Joffre delivered his counter-stroke on the 7th of September.

Sir John French describes only the operations of the British Force and of the two French armies which covered its flanks—the Sixth Army on his left, and the Fifth on his right. These three armies were drawn up on the 6th of September along an arc of a circle, extending from Betz to Meaux, and thence behind the Grand Morin River to Esternay. Their attack was mainly di-

Field-Marshal Sir John French

FIELD-MARSHAL SIR DOUGLAS HAIG

rected against the 1st German Army, which now extended from the Ourcq to various points south of the Grand Morin, though the 2nd German Army, further to the east, also came into action against the right of the 5th French Army.

The object of the Allies was to isolate the 1st German Army and thrust it northwards. The 6th French Army moved eastward against the line of the Ourcq; the British troops and the 5th French Army moved north in the direction of the Marne. They found the enemy aware of their intention and already on the retreat; from the 7th of September to the 10th inclusive the three allied armies were in hot pursuit, and continually engaged with the German rearguards, whose positions originally extended from the east of the Ourcq to various points south-west of Montmirail. These engagements took place in a region which is intersected by the Marne and its tributaries, by the southern tributaries of the Aisne, and by a number of canals. The general plan of the German rearguards was to hold the fords and bridges of these waterways.

Our Force now contained three Army Corps and was therefore stronger than it had been at Mons. It crossed the Grand Morin, apparently without serious difficulty, on the 7th of September; on the 8th it forced the passage of the Petit Morin after severe fighting; on the 9th it carried the Marne between La Ferté and the confluence of the Ourcq; on the 10th it was pursuing the enemy up the east bank of the Ourcq in the direction of Soissons. Further to the east the 6th French Army was advancing northwards in the same manner. On the 11th the British Force was south and south-east of Soissons facing the Aisne. At this point the German 1st and 2nd Armies ceased their retreat; the 1st Army was in position between Missy and Villers, to the north of the Aisne; the 2nd Army was north of Reims.

The Battle of the Aisne is clearly described by Sir John French. It opened on the 13th of September with British attacks upon three points of the Aisne between Soissons and Villers. The 3rd Army Corps (under Lieut.-General Pulteney) was on the extreme left; it attacked the line of the river at Soissons and also at Venizel, which is about four miles east of Soissons; the 2nd Corps attacked opposite Missy, to the east of Venizel; the 1st Corps advanced on a line reaching from Chavonne on the west to Bourg on the east. All the three Corps had established a footing on the north bank of the Aisne by nightfall. They had also begun to force their way up the high ground on which the Germans were entrenched. The Germans therefore withdrew to the high ridge two miles north of the river and parallel with it, along which runs the road called Chemin des Dames (through Courtecon and north of Ostel).

The British forces spent the 14th of September in bridging the Aisne and strengthening the positions already gained. On the 15th the 1st Corps, under Sir Douglas Haig, advanced from the right of the British position, covering the line from Moulins on the east to Ostel on the west. Their object was to outflank the enemy and drive him north-west; and by the end of the day Sir Douglas Haig had so far succeeded that his right flank touched the Chemin des Dames at a point near Courtecon. But the enemy had now brought up their heavy guns from the siege of Maubeuge; and, for the following days of the battle, Sir Douglas Haig could only hold the position which he had won.

Sir John French received information that the enemy was making a stand in force along the whole line of high ground from the north of Compiègne to the north of Reims. He also learned from General Joffre that the decisive attack was to be delivered by French armies on the left of the Allied position. Accordingly, from the 16th to the 28th, the British forces made no attempt to carry out extensive attacking movements. They entrenched themselves, and were for the most part engaged in repelling attacks of extraordinary violence, which reached their culmination on the 26th, 27th, and 28th.

The advance to the Aisne and the Battle of the Aisne have not the dramatic interest which attaches to the retreat from Mons; in September the British forces were acting in close co-operation with French armies, and were no longer threatened by overwhelming odds. But the second "eyewitness" report which we

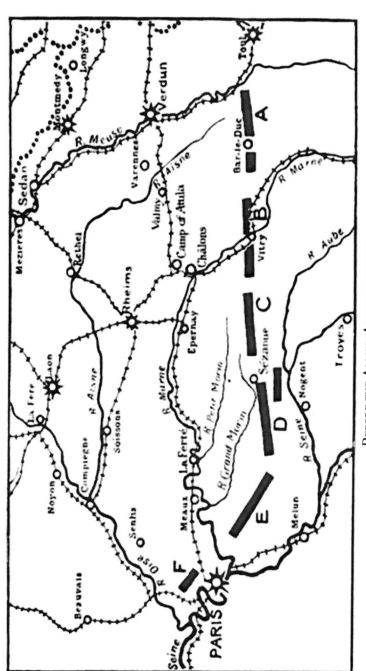

BEFORE THE ALLIED ARMIES ADVANCE

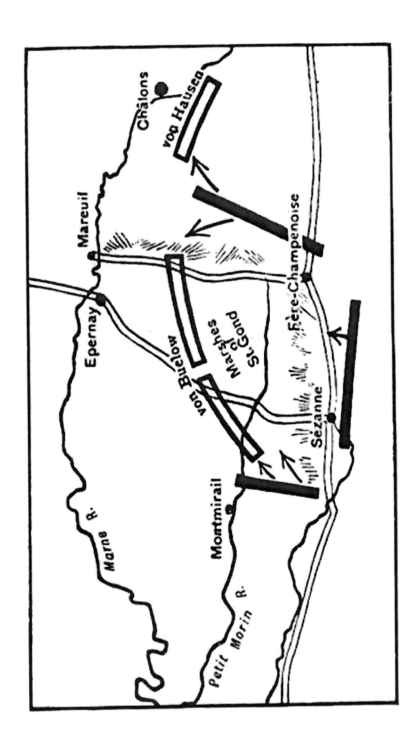

Châlons

von Hausen

Mareuil

Épernay

Marne R.

von Buelow

Marshes of St-Gond

Fère-Champenoise

Sézanne

Montmirail

Petit Morin R.

print below (Appendix B) shows, even better than the dispatches of the Commander-in-Chief, how desperate was the fighting on the Aisne. The advance of Sir Douglas Haig to the Chemin des Dames, and his obstinate defence of the valuable strategic points which he thereby secured, must rank among the most splendid feats of gallantry and endurance which have been witnessed in the western theatre of the war.

Despatches

1

17th September, 1914.

My Lord,

In continuation of my despatch of September 7th, I have the honour to report the further progress of the operations of the Forces under my command from August 28th,

Retreat to the Line Compiègne-Soissons

On that evening the retirement of the Force was followed closely by two of the enemy's cavalry columns, moving south-east from St. Quentin.

The retreat in this part of the field was being covered by the Third and Fifth Cavalry Brigades. South of the Somme General Gough, with the Third Cavalry Brigade, threw back the *Uhlans* of the Guard with considerable loss.

General Chetwode, with the Fifth Cavalry Brigade, encountered the eastern column near Cérizy, moving south. The Brigade attacked and routed the column, the leading German regiment suffering very severe casualties and being almost broken up.

The 7th French Army Corps was now in course of being railed up from the south to the east of Amiens. On the 29th it nearly completed its detrainment, and the French 6th Army got into position on my left, its right resting on Roye.

The 5th French Army was behind the line of the Oise between La Fère and Guise.

The pursuit of the enemy was very vigorous; some five or six German corps were on the Somme, facing the 5th Army on the Oise. At least two corps were advancing towards my front, and were crossing the Somme east and west of Ham. Three or four more German corps were opposing the 6th French Army on my left.

This was the situation at 1 o'clock on the 29th, when I received a visit from General Joffre at my headquarters.

I strongly represented my position to the French Commander-in-Chief, who was most kind, cordial, and sympathetic, as he has always been. He told me that he had directed the 5th French Army on the Oise to move forward and attack the Germans on the Somme, with a view to checking pursuit. He also told me of the formation of the 6th French Army on my left flank, composed of the 7th Army Corps, four Reserve Divisions, and Sordêt's Corps of Cavalry.

I finally arranged with General Joffre to effect a further short retirement towards the line Compiègne-Soissons, promising him, however, to do my utmost to keep always within a day's march of him.

In pursuance of this arrangement the British Forces retired to a position a few miles north of the line Compiègne-Soissons on the 29th.

The right flank of the German Army was now reaching a point which appeared seriously to endanger my line of communications with Havre.

I had already evacuated Amiens, into which place a German reserve division was reported to have moved.

Orders were given to change the base to St. Nazaire, and establish an advance base at Le Mans. This operation was well carried out by the Inspector-General of Communications.

In spite of a severe defeat inflicted upon the Guard 10th and Guard Reserve Corps of the German Army by the 1st and 3rd French Corps on the right of the 5th Army, it was not part of General Joffre's plan to pursue this advantage; and a general retirement on to the line of the Marne was ordered, to which the French Forces in the more eastern theatre were directed to conform.

A new Army (the 9th) had been formed from three corps in the south by General Joffre, and moved into the space between the right of the 5th and left of the 4th Armies.

Whilst closely adhering to his strategic conception to draw the enemy on at all points until a favourable situation was created from which to assume the offensive, General Joffre found it necessary to modify from day to day the methods by which he sought to attain this object, owing to the development of the enemy's plans and changes in the general situation.

In conformity with the movements of the French Forces, my retirement continued practically from day to day. Although we were not severely pressed by the enemy, rearguard actions took place continually.

RETREAT FROM THE AISNE TO THE MARNE

On the 1st September, when retiring from the thickly wooded country to the south of Compiègne, the First Cavalry Brigade was overtaken by some German cavalry. They momentarily lost a Horse Artillery battery, and several officers and men were killed and wounded. With the help, however, of some detachments from the 3rd Corps operating on their left, they not only recovered their own guns but succeeded in capturing twelve of the enemy's.

Similarly, to the eastward, the 1st Corps, retiring south, also got into some very difficult forest country, and a somewhat severe rearguard action ensued at Villers-Cotterets, in which the Fourth Guards Brigade suffered considerably.

On September 3rd the British Forces were in position south of the Marne between Lagny and Signy-Signets. Up to this time I had been requested by General Joffre

GENERAL JOSEPH JOFFRE

GERMAN INFANTRY ADVANCE

to defend the passages of the river as long as possible, and to blow up the bridges in my front. After I had made the necessary dispositions, and the destruction of the bridges had been effected, I was asked by the French Commander-in-Chief to continue my retirement to a point some 12 miles in rear of the position I then occupied, with a view to taking up a second position behind the Seine. This retirement was duly carried out. In the meantime the enemy had thrown bridges and crossed the Marne in considerable force, and was threatening the Allies all along the line of the British Forces and the 5th and 9th French Armies, Consequently several small outpost actions took place.

Preparations for the Counter-Advance

On Saturday, September 5th, I met the French Commander-in-Chief at his request, and he informed me of his intention to take the offensive forthwith, as he considered conditions were very favourable to success.

General Joffre announced to me his intention of wheeling up the left flank of the 6th Army, pivoting on the Marne and directing it to move on the Ourcq; cross and attack the flank of the 1st German Army, which was then moving in a south-easterly direction east of that river.

He requested me to effect a change of front to my right—my left resting on the Marne and my right on the 5th Army—to fill the gap between that army and the 6th. I was then to advance against the enemy in my front and join in the general offensive movement.

These combined movements practically commenced on Sunday, September 6th, at sunrise; and on that day it may be said that a great battle opened on a front extending from Ermenonville, which was just in front of the left flank of the 6th French Army, through Lizy on the Marne, Mauperthuis, which was about the British centre, Courtecon, which was the left of the 5th French Army, to Es-

25

ternay and Charleville, the left of the 9th Army under General Foch, and so along the front of the 9th, 4th, and 3rd French Armies to a point north of the fortress of Verdun.

This battle, in so far as the 6th French Army, the British Army, the 5th French Army and the 9th French Army were concerned, may be said to have concluded on the evening of September 10th, by which time the Germans had been driven back to the line Soissons-Reims, with a loss of thousands of prisoners, many guns, and enormous masses of transport.

THE GERMAN RIGHT WING SWERVES SOUTH-EAST

About the 3rd September the enemy appears to have changed his plans and to have determined to stop his advance South direct upon Paris; for on the 4th September air reconnaissances showed that his main columns were moving in a south-easterly direction generally east of a line drawn through Nanteuil and Lizy on the Ourcq.

On the 5th September several of these columns were observed to have crossed the Marne; whilst German troops, which were observed moving south-east up the left bank of the Ourcq on the 4th, were now reported to be halted and facing that river. Heads of the enemy's columns were seen crossing at Changis, La Ferté, Nogent, Château Thierry and Mezy.

Considerable German columns of all arms were seen to be converging on Montmirail, whilst before sunset large bivouacs of the enemy were located in the neighbourhood of Coulommiers, south of Rebais, La Ferté-Gaucher and Lagny.

COUNTER-ADVANCE OF THE ALLIED LEFT

I should conceive it to have been about noon on the 6th September, after the British Forces had changed their front to the right and occupied the line Jouy-Le Chatel-Faremoutiers-Villeneuve Le Comte, and the advance of the 6th French Army north of the Marne towards the Ourcq became apparent, that the enemy realised the powerful threat that was being made against the flank of his columns moving south-east, and began the great retreat which opened the battle above referred to.

On the evening of the 6th September, therefore, the fronts and positions of the opposing armies were roughly as follows:

ALLIES.

6th French Army.—Right on the Marne at Meaux, left towards Betz.

British Forces.—On the line Dagny-Coulommiers-Maison.

5th French Army.—At Courtaçon, right on Esternay.

Conneau's Cavalry Corps.—Between the right of the British and the left of the French 5th Army.

GERMANS.

4th Reserve and 2nd Corps.—East of the Ourcq and facing that river.

9th Cavalry Division.—West of Crecy.

2nd Cavalry Division.—North of Coulommiers.

4th Corps.—Rebais.

3rd and 7th Corps.—South-west of Montmirail.

All these troops constituted the 1st German Army, which was directed against the French 6th Army on the Ourcq, and the British Forces, and the left of the 5th French Army south of the Marne,

The 2nd German Army (9th, 10th, 10th R. and Guard) was moving against the centre and right of the 5th French Army and the 9th French Army.

STAGES OF THE ADVANCE, SEPT. 7-9

On the 7th September both the 5th and 6th French Armies were heavily engaged on our flank. The 2nd and 4th

Reserve German Corps on the Ourcq vigorously opposed the advance of the French towards that river, but did not prevent the 6th Army from gaining some headway, the Germans themselves suffering serious losses. The French 5th Army threw the enemy back to the line of the Petit Morin river after inflicting severe losses upon them, especially about Montceaux, which was carried at the point of the bayonet.

The enemy retreated before our advance, covered by his 2nd and 9th and Guard Cavalry Divisions, which suffered severely.

Our Cavalry acted with great vigour, especially General De Lisle's Brigade with the 9th Lancers and 18th Hussars,

On the 8th September the enemy continued his retreat northward, and our Army was successfully engaged during the day with strong rearguards of all arms on the Petit Morin River, thereby materially assisting the progress of the French Armies on our right and left, against whom the enemy was making his greatest efforts. On both sides the enemy was thrown back with very heavy loss. The First Army Corps encountered stubborn resistance at La Trétoire (north of Rebais). The enemy occupied a strong position with infantry and guns on the northern bank of the Petit Morin River; they were dislodged with considerable loss. Several machine guns and many prisoners were captured, and upwards of two hundred German dead were left on the ground.

The forcing of the Petit Morin at this point was much assisted by the Cavalry and the 1st Division, which crossed higher up the stream.

Later in the day a counter-attack by the enemy was well repulsed by the First Army Corps, a great many prisoners and some guns again falling into our hands.

On this day (8th September) the Second Army Corps encountered considerable opposition, but drove back the

BRITISH SOLDIERS UNDER FIRE FROM GERMAN ARTILLERY

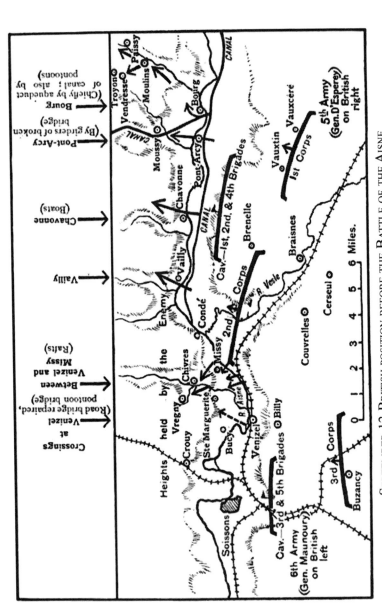

SEPTEMBER 12-BRITISH POSITION BEFORE THE BATTLE OF THE AISNE

enemy at all points with great loss, making considerable captures.

The Third Army Corps also drove back considerable bodies of the enemy's infantry and made some captures.

On the 9th September the First and Second Army Corps forced the passage of the Marne and advanced some miles to the north of it. The Third Corps encountered considerable opposition, as the bridge at La Ferté was destroyed and the enemy held the town on the opposite bank in some strength, and thence persistently obstructed the construction of a bridge; so the passage was not effected until after nightfall.

During the day's pursuit the enemy suffered heavy loss in killed and wounded, some hundreds of prisoners fell into our hands, and a battery of eight machine guns was captured by the 2nd Division.

On this day the 6th French Army was heavily engaged west of the River Ourcq. The enemy had largely increased his force opposing them; and very heavy fighting ensued, in which the French were successful throughout.

The left of the 5th French Army reached the neighbourhood of Château Thierry after the most severe fighting, having driven the enemy completely north of the river with great loss.

THE BRITISH ON THE OURCQ, SEPT. 10

The fighting of this Army in the neighbourhood of Montmirail was very severe.

The advance was resumed at daybreak on the 10th up to the line of the Ourcq, opposed by strong rearguards of all arms. The 1st and 2nd Corps, assisted by the Cavalry Division on the right, the 3rd and 5th Cavalry Brigades on the left, drove the enemy northwards. Thirteen guns, seven machine guns, about 2,000 prisoners, and quantities of transport fell into our hands. The enemy left many dead on the field. On this day the French 5th and 6th Armies had little opposition.

As the 1st and 2nd German Armies were now in full retreat, this evening marks the end of the battle which practically commenced on the morning of the 6th instant; and it is at this point in the operations that I am concluding the present despatch.

Although I deeply regret to have had to report heavy losses in killed and wounded throughout these operations, I do not think they have been excessive in view of the magnitude of the great fight, the outlines of which I have only been able very briefly to describe, and the demoralisation and loss in killed and wounded which are known to have been caused to the enemy by the vigour and severity of the pursuit.

In concluding this despatch I must call your Lordship's special attention to the fact that from Sunday, August 23rd, up to the present date (September 17th), from Mons back almost to the Seine, and from the Seine to the Aisne, the Army under my command has been ceaselessly engaged without one single day's halt or rest of any kind.

Since the date to which in this despatch I have limited my report of the operations, a great battle on the Aisne has been proceeding. A full report of this battle will be made in an early further despatch.

It will, however, be of interest to say here that, in spite of a very determined resistance on the part of the enemy, who is holding in strength and great tenacity a position peculiarly favourable to defence, the battle which commenced on the evening of the 12th instant has, so far, forced the enemy back from his first position, secured the passage of the river, and inflicted great loss upon him, including the capture of over 2,000 prisoners and several guns.

I have the honour to be,

Your Lordship's most obedient Servant,

(Signed) J. D. P. French, Field-Marshal,

Commanding-in-Chief, the British Forces in the Field.

8th October, 1914.

My Lord,

I have the honour to report the operations in which the British Forces in France have been engaged since the evening of the 10th September.

FROM THE OURCQ TO THE AISNE

1. In the early morning of the 11th the further pursuit of the enemy was commenced; and the three Corps crossed the Ourcq practically unopposed, the Cavalry reaching the line of the Aisne River; the 3rd and 5th Brigades south of Soissons, the 1st, 2nd and 4th on the high ground at Couvrelles and Cerseuil.

On the afternoon of the 12th from the opposition encountered by the 6th French Army to the west of Soissons, by the 3rd Corps south-east of that place, by the 2nd Corps south of Missy and Vailly, and certain indications all along the line, I formed the opinion that the enemy had, for the moment at any rate, arrested his retreat and was preparing to dispute the passage of the Aisne with some vigour.

South of Soissons the Germans were holding Mont de Paris against the attack of the right of the French 6th Army when the 3rd Corps reached the neighbourhood of Buzancy, south-east of that place. With the assistance of the Artillery of the 3rd Corps the French drove them back across the river at Soissons, where they destroyed the bridges.

The heavy artillery fire which was visible for several miles in a westerly direction in the valley of the Aisne showed that the 6th French Army was meeting with strong opposition all along the line.

On this day the Cavalry under General Allenby reached the neighbourhood of Braine and did good work in clearing the town and the high ground beyond it of strong hostile detachments. The Queen's Bays are particularly mentioned by the General as having assisted greatly in the success of this operation. They were well supported by the 3rd Division, which on this night bivouacked at Brenelle, south of the river.

The 5th Division approached Missy, but were unable to make headway.

The 1st Army Corps reached the neighbourhood of Vaux-céré without much opposition.

In this manner the Battle of the Aisne commenced.

2. The Aisne Valley runs generally East and West, and consists of a flat-bottomed depression of width varying from half a mile to two miles, down which the river follows a winding course to the West at some points near the southern slopes of the valley and at others near the northern. The high ground both on the north and south of the river is approximately 400 feet above the bottom of the valley and is very similar in character, as are both slopes of the valley itself, which are broken into numerous rounded spurs and re-entrants. The most prominent of the former are the Chivre spur on the right bank and Sermoise spur on the left.

Near the latter place the general *plateau* on the south is divided by a subsidiary valley of much the same character, down which the small River Vesle flows to the main stream near Sermoise. The slopes of the *plateau* overlooking the Aisne on the north and south are of varying steepness, and are covered with numerous patches of wood, which also stretch upwards and backwards over the edge on to the top of the high ground. There are several villages and small towns dotted about in the valley itself and along its sides, the chief of which is the town of Soissons.

The Aisne is a sluggish stream of some 170 feet in breadth, but, being 16 feet deep in the centre, it is unfordable. Be-

The French on the Firing Line

THE FRENCH RETAKING A VILLAGE

tween Soissons on the west and Villers on the east (the part of the river attacked and secured by the British Forces) there are eleven road bridges across it. On the north bank a narrow-gauge railway runs from Soissons to Vailly, where it crosses the river and continues eastward along the south bank. From Soissons to Sermoise a double line of railway runs along the south bank, turning at the latter place up the Vesle Valley towards Bazoches,

The position held by the enemy is a very strong one, either for a delaying action or for a defensive battle. One of its chief military characteristics is that from the high ground on neither side can the top of the *plateau* on the other side be seen except for small stretches. This is chiefly due to the woods on the edges of the slopes. Another important point is that all the bridges are under either direct or high-angle artillery fire.

The tract of country above described, which lies north of the Aisne, is well adapted to concealment, and was so skilfully turned to account by the enemy as to render it impossible to judge the real nature of his opposition to our passage of the river, or to accurately gauge his strength; but I have every reason to conclude that strong rearguards of at least three army corps were holding the passages on the early morning of the 13th.

PASSAGE OF THE AISNE, SEPT. 13

3. On that morning I ordered the British Forces to advance and make good the Aisne.

The 1st Corps and the Cavalry advanced on the river. The 1st Division was directed on Chanouille *via* the canal bridge at Bourg, and the 2nd Division on Courtecon and Presles *via* Pont-Arcy and on the canal to the north of Braye *via* Chavonne. On the right the Cavalry and 1st Division met with slight opposition, and found a passage by means of the canal which crosses the river by an aqueduct. The Division was therefore able to press on, supported by the Cavalry Division on its outer flank, driving back the enemy in front of it.

On the left the leading troops of the 2nd Division reached the river by 9 o'clock. The 5th Infantry Brigade were only enabled to cross, in single file and under considerable shell fire, by means of the broken girder of the bridge which was not entirely submerged in the river. The construction of a pontoon bridge was at once undertaken, and was completed by 5 o'clock in the afternoon.

On the extreme left the 4th Guards Brigade met with severe opposition at Chavonne, and it was only late in the afternoon that it was able to establish a foothold on the northern bank of the river by ferrying one battalion across in boats.

By nightfall the 1st Division occupied the area Moulins Paissy-Geny, with posts in the village of Vendresse.

The 2nd Division bivouacked as a whole on the southern bank of the river, leaving only the 5th Brigade on the north bank to establish a bridge head.

The Second Corps found all the bridges in front of them destroyed, except that of Condé, which was in possession of the enemy, and remained so until the end of the battle. In the approach to Missy, where the 5th Division eventually crossed, there is some open ground which was swept by heavy fire from the opposite bank. The 13th Brigade was, therefore, unable to advance; but the 14th, which was directed to the east of Venizel at a less exposed point, was rafted across, and by night established itself with its left at St. Marguérite. They were followed by the 15th Brigade; and later on both the 14th and 15th supported the 4th Division on their left in repelling a heavy counter-attack on the Third Corps.

On the morning of the 13th the Third Corps found the enemy had established himself in strength on the Vregny Plateau. The road bridge at Venizel was repaired during the morning, and a reconnaissance was made with a view to throwing a pontoon bridge at Soissons.

The 12th Infantry Brigade crossed at Venizel, and was assembled at Bucy Le Long by 1 p.m., but the bridge was so far damaged that artillery could only be man-handled across it. Meanwhile the construction of a bridge was commenced close to the road bridge at Venizel.

At 2 p.m. the 12th Infantry Brigade attacked in the direction of Chivres and Vregny with the object of securing the high ground east of Chivres, as a necessary preliminary to a further advance northwards. This attack made good progress, but at 5.30 p.m. the enemy's artillery and machine-gun fire from the direction of Vregny became so severe that no further advance could be made. The positions reached were held till dark.

The pontoon bridge at Venizel was completed at 6.30 p.m., when the 10th Infantry Brigade crossed the river and moved to Bucy Le Long.

The 19th Infantry Brigade moved to Billy-sur-Aisne, and before dark all the artillery of the Division had crossed the river, with the exception of the Heavy Battery and one Brigade of Field Artillery.

During the night the positions gained by the 12th Infantry Brigade to the east of the stream running through Chivres were handed over to the 5th Division.

The section of the Bridging Train allotted to the Third Corps began to arrive in the neighbourhood of Soissons late in the afternoon, when an attempt to throw a heavy pontoon bridge at Soissons had to be abandoned, owing to the fire of the enemy's heavy howitzers.

In the evening the enemy retired at all points and entrenched himself on the high ground about two miles north of the river along which runs the Chemin-des-Dames. Detachments of Infantry, however, strongly entrenched in commanding points down slopes of the various spurs, were left in front of all three corps with powerful artillery in support of them.

During the night of the 13th and on the 14th and following days the Field Companies were incessantly at work night and day. Eight pontoon bridges and one foot bridge were thrown across the river under generally very heavy artillery fire, which was incessantly kept up on to most of the crossings after completion. Three of the road bridges, *i.e.* Venizel, Missy and Vailly, and the railway bridge east of Vailly were temporarily repaired so as to take foot traffic, and the Villers Bridge made fit to carry weights up to six tons.

Preparations were also made for the repair of the Missy, Vailly and Bourg Bridges so as to take mechanical transport.

The weather was very wet and added to the difficulties by cutting up the already indifferent approaches, entailing a large amount of work to repair and improve.

The operations of the Field Companies during this most trying time are worthy of the best traditions of the Royal Engineers.

THE ADVANCE OF THE FIRST CORPS
(SIR DOUGLAS HAIG)

4. On the evening of the 14th it was still impossible to decide whether the enemy was only making a temporary halt, covered by rearguards, or whether he intended to stand and defend the position.

With a view to clearing up the situation, I ordered a general advance.

The action of the First Corps on this day under the direction and command of Sir Douglas Haig was of so skilful, bold and decisive a character that he gained positions which alone have enabled me to maintain my position for more than three weeks of very severe fighting on the north bank of the river.

The Corps was directed to cross the line Moulins–Moussy by 7 a.m.

On the right the General Officer Commanding the 1st Division directed the 2nd Infantry Brigade (which was in billets and bivouacked about Moulins) and the 25th Artillery Brigade (less one battery), under General Bulfin, to move forward before daybreak, in order to protect the advance of the Division sent up the valley to Vendresse. An officers' patrol sent out by this Brigade reported a considerable force of the enemy near the factory north of Troyon, and the Brigadier accordingly directed two regiments (the King's Royal Rifles and the Royal Sussex Regiment) to move at 3 a.m. The Northamptonshire Regiment was ordered to move at 4 a.m. to occupy the spur east of Troyon.

The remaining regiment of the Brigade (the Loyal North Lancashire Regiment) moved at 5.30 a.m. to the village of Vendresse. The factory was found to be held in considerable strength by the enemy, and the Brigadier ordered the Loyal North Lancashire Regiment to support the King's Royal Rifles and the Sussex Regiment. Even with this support the force was unable to make headway, and on the arrival of the 1st Brigade the Coldstream Guards were moved up to support the right of the leading Brigade (the 2nd), while the remainder of the 1st Brigade supported its left.

About noon the situation was, roughly, that the whole of these two brigades were extended along a line running east and west, north of the line Troy on and south of the Chemin-des-Dames. A party of the Loyal North Lancashire Regiment had seized and were holding the factory. The enemy held a line of entrenchments north and east of the factory in considerable strength, and every effort to advance against this line was driven back by heavy shell and machine-gun fire. The morning was wet and a heavy mist hung over the hills, so that the 25th Artillery Brigade and the Divisional Artillery were unable to render effective support to the advanced troops until about 9 o'clock.

By 10 o'clock the 3rd Infantry Brigade had reached a point one mile south of Vendresse, and from there it was ordered to continue the line of the 1st Brigade and to connect with and help the right of the 2nd Division. A strong hostile column was found to be advancing, and by a vigorous counter-stroke with two of his battalions the Brigadier checked the advance of this column and relieved the pressure on the 2nd Division. From this period until late in the afternoon the fighting consisted of a series of attacks and counter-attacks. The counter-strokes by the enemy were delivered at first with great vigour, but later on they decreased in strength, and all were driven off with heavy loss.

On the left the 6th Infantry Brigade had been ordered to cross the river and to pass through the line held during the preceding night by the 5th Infantry Brigade and occupy the Courtecon Ridge, whilst a detached force, consisting of the 4th Guards Brigade and the 36th Brigade, Royal Field Artillery, under Brigadier-General Perceval, were ordered to proceed to a point east of the village of Ostel.

The 6th Infantry Brigade crossed the river at Pont-Arcy, moved up the valley towards Braye, and at 9 a.m. had reached the line Tilleul-La Buvelle. On this line they came under heavy artillery and rifle fire, and were unable to advance until supported by the 34th Brigade, Royal Field Artillery, and the 44th Howitzer Brigade and the Heavy Artillery.

The 4th Guards Brigade crossed the river at 10 a.m. and met with very heavy opposition. It had to pass through dense woods; field artillery support was difficult to obtain; but one section of a field battery pushed up to and within the firing line. At 1 p.m. the left of the Brigade was south of the Ostel Ridge.

At this period of the action the enemy obtained a footing between the First and Second Corps, and threatened to cut the communications of the latter.

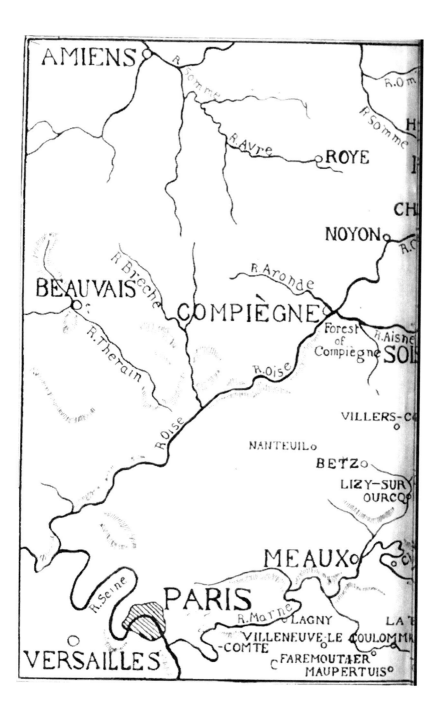

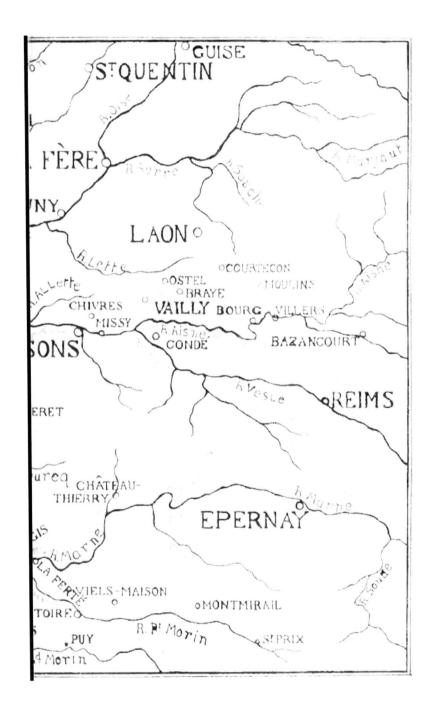

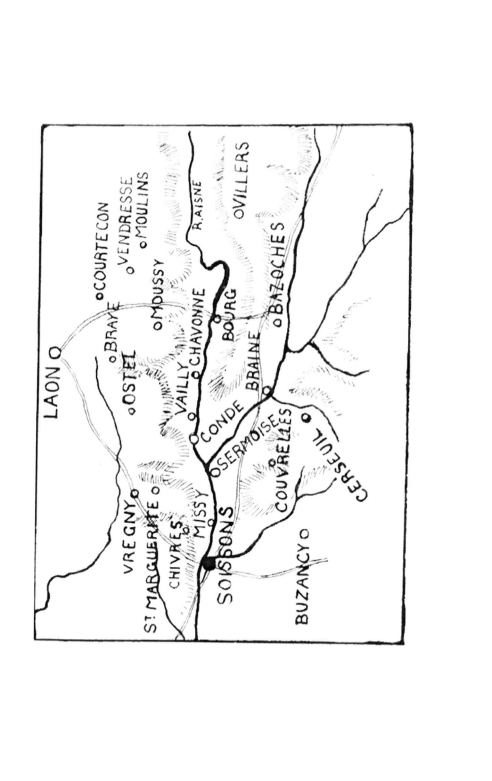

MAUBEUGE FORTRESS

MAUBEUGE FORTRESS

GERMAN PRISONERS OF WAR FROM MAUBEUGE

Sir Douglas Haig was very hardly pressed and had no reserve in hand. I placed the Cavalry Division at his disposal, part of which he skilfully used to prolong and secure the left flank of the Guards Brigade. Some heavy fighting ensued, which resulted in the enemy being driven back with heavy loss.

About 4 o'clock the weakening of the counter-attacks by the enemy and other indications tended to show that his resistance was decreasing, and a general advance was ordered by the Army Corps Commander. Although meeting with considerable opposition and coming under very heavy artillery and rifle fire, the position of the corps at the end of the day's operations extended from the Chemin-des-Dames on the right, through Chivy, to Le Cour de Soupir, with the 1st Cavalry Brigade extending to the Chavonne-Soissons road.

On the right the corps was in close touch with the French Moroccan troops of the 18th Corps, which were entrenched in *échelon* to its right rear. During the night they entrenched this position.

Throughout the Battle of the Aisne this advanced and commanding position was maintained, and I cannot speak too highly of the valuable services rendered by Sir Douglas Haig and the Army Corps under his command. Day after day and night after night the enemy's infantry has been hurled against him in violent counter-attack which has never on any one occasion succeeded, whilst the trenches all over his position have been under continuous heavy artillery fire.

The operations of the First Corps on this day resulted in the capture of several hundred prisoners, some field pieces, and machine guns.

The casualties were very severe, one brigade alone losing three of its four colonels.

The 3rd Division commenced a further advance and had nearly reached the *plateau* of Aizy when they were driven back by a powerful counter-attack supported by heavy artillery. The division, however, fell back in the best order, and finally entrenched itself about a mile north of Vailly Bridge, effectively covering the passage.

The 4th and 5th Divisions were unable to do more than maintain their ground.

THE GERMAN HEAVY GUNS, SEPT. 15

5. On the morning of the 15th, after close examination of the position, it became clear to me that the enemy was making a determined stand; and this view was confirmed by reports which reached me from the French Armies fighting on my right and left, which clearly showed that a strongly entrenched line of defence was being taken up from the north of Compiègne, eastward and south-eastward, along the whole valley of the Aisne up to and beyond Reims.

A few days previously the Fortress of Maubeuge fell, and a considerable quantity of siege artillery was brought down from that place to strengthen the enemy's position in front of us.

During the 15th shells fell in our position which have been judged by experts to be thrown by eight-inch siege guns with a range of 10,000 yards. Throughout the whole course of the battle our troops have suffered very heavily from this fire, although its effect latterly was largely mitigated by more efficient and thorough entrenching, the necessity for which I impressed strongly upon Army Corps Commanders. In order to assist them in this work all villages within the area of our occupation were searched for heavy entrenching tools, a large number of which were collected.

In view of the peculiar formation of the ground on the north side of the river between Missy and Soissons, and its extraordinary adaptability to a force on the defensive, the 5th Division found it impossible to maintain its position on the southern edge of the Chivres Plateau, as the enemy in possession of the village of Vregny to the west was able to bring a flank fire to bear upon it. The Division had, therefore, to retire to a line the left of which was at the village of Marguerite, and thence ran by the north edge of Missy back to the river to the east of that place.

With great skill and tenacity Sir Charles Fergusson maintained this position throughout the whole battle, although his trenches were necessarily on lower ground than that occupied by the enemy on the southern edge of the plateau, which was only 400 yards away.

General Hamilton with the 3rd Division vigorously attacked to the north, and regained all the ground he had lost on the 15th, which throughout the battle has formed a most powerful and effective bridge head.

ATTACKS AND COUNTER-ATTACKS
SEPT. 16-24

6. On the 16th the 6th Division came up into line.

It had been my intention to direct the First Corps to attack and seize the enemy's position on the Chemin-des-Dames, supporting it with this new reinforcement. I hoped from the position thus gained to bring effective fire to bear across the front of the 3rd Division which, by securing the advance of the latter, would also take the pressure off the 6th Division and the Third Corps.

But any further advance of the First Corps would have dangerously exposed my right flank. And, further, I learned from the French Commander-in-Chief that he was strongly reinforcing the 6th French Army on my left, with the intention of bringing up the Allied left to attack the enemy's flank and thus compel his retirement. I therefore sent the 6th Division to join the Third Corps with orders to keep it on the south side of the river, as it might be available in general reserve.

On the 17th, 18th and 19th the whole of our line was

heavily bombarded, and the First Corps was constantly and heavily engaged. On the afternoon of the 17th the right flank of the 1st Division was seriously threatened. A counter-attack was made by the Northamptonshire Regiment in combination with the Queen's, and one battalion of the Divisional Reserve was moved up in support. The Northamptonshire Regiment, under cover of mist, crept up to within a hundred yards of the enemy's trenches and charged with the bayonet, driving them out of the trenches and up the hill.

A very strong force of hostile infantry was then disclosed on the crest line. This new line was enfiladed by part of the Queen's and the King's Royal Rifles, which wheeled to their left on the extreme right of our infantry line, and were supported by a squadron of cavalry on their outer flank. The enemy's attack was ultimately driven back with heavy loss.

On the 18th, during the night, the Gloucestershire Regiment advanced from their position near Chivy, filled in the enemy's trenches and captured two maxim guns.

On the extreme right the Queen's were heavily attacked, but the enemy was repulsed with great loss. About midnight the attack was renewed on the First Division, supported by artillery fire, but was again repulsed.

Shortly after midnight an attack was made on the left of the 2nd Division with considerable force, which was also thrown back.

At about 1 p.m. on the 19th the 2nd Division drove back a heavy infantry attack strongly supported by artillery fire. At dusk the attack was renewed and again repulsed.

On the 18th I discussed with the General Officer Commanding the Second Army Corps and his Divisional Commanders the possibility of driving the enemy out of Condé, which lay between his two Divisions, and seizing the bridge which has remained throughout in his possession.

As, however, I found that the bridge was closely commanded from all points on the south side and that satisfactory arrangements were made to prevent any issue from it by the enemy by day or night, I decided that it was not necessary to incur the losses which an attack would entail, as, in view of the position of the Second and Third Corps, the enemy could make no use of Condé, and would be automatically forced out of it by any advance which might become possible for us.

7. On this day information reached me from General Joffre that he had found it necessary to make a new plan, and to attack and envelop the German right flank.

It was now evident to me that the battle in which we had been engaged since the 12th instant must last some days longer until the effect of this new flank movement could be felt and a way opened to drive the enemy from his positions.

It thus became essential to establish some system of regular relief in the trenches, and I have used the infantry of the 6th Division for this purpose with good results. The relieved brigades were brought back alternately south of the river, and, with the artillery of the 6th Division, formed a general reserve on which I could rely in case of necessity. The Cavalry has rendered most efficient and ready help in the trenches, and have done all they possibly could to lighten the arduous and trying task which has of necessity fallen to the lot of the Infantry.

On the evening of the 19th and throughout the 20th the enemy again commenced to show considerable activity. On the former night a severe counter-attack on the 3rd Division was repulsed with considerable loss, and from early on Sunday morning various hostile attempts were made on the trenches of the 1st Division. During the day the enemy suffered another severe repulse in front of the 2nd Division, losing heavily in the attempt. In the course of the afternoon the enemy made desperate attempts against the trenches all along the front of the First Corps, but with similar results.

After dark the enemy again attacked the 2nd Division, only to be again driven back.

Our losses on these two days were considerable, but the number, as obtained, of the enemy's killed and wounded vastly exceeded them.

As the troops of the First Army Corps were much exhausted by this continual fighting, I reinforced Sir Douglas Haig with a brigade from the reserve, and called upon the 1st Cavalry Division to assist them.

On the night of the 21st another violent counter-attack was repulsed by the 3rd Division, the enemy losing heavily.

On the 23rd the four six-inch howitzer batteries, which I had asked to be sent from home, arrived. Two batteries were handed over to the Second Corps and two to the First Corps. They were brought into action on the 24th with very good results.

Our experiences in this campaign seem to point to the employment of more heavy guns of a larger calibre in great battles which last for several days, during which time powerful entrenching work on both sides can be carried out.

These batteries were used with considerable effect on the 24th and the following days.

CLIMAX OF GERMAN COUNTER-ATTACKS
SEPT. 26-28

8. On the 23rd the action of General de Castelnau's Army on the Allied left developed considerably, and apparently withdrew considerable forces of the enemy away from the centre and east. I am not aware whether it was due to this cause or not, but until the 26th it appeared as though the enemy's opposition in our front was weakening. On that day, however, a very marked renewal of activity com-

menced. A constant and vigorous artillery bombardment was maintained all day, and the Germans in front of the 1st Division were observed to be "sapping" up to our lines and trying to establish new trenches. Renewed counter-attacks were delivered and beaten off during the course of the day, and in the afternoon a well-timed attack by the 1st Division stopped the enemy's entrenching work.

During the night of 27th-28th the enemy again made the most determined attempts to capture the trenches of the 1st Division, but without the slightest success.

Similar attacks were reported during these three days all along the line of the Allied front, and it is certain that the enemy then made one last great effort to establish ascendancy. He was, however, unsuccessful everywhere, and is reported to have suffered heavy losses. The same futile attempts were made all along our front up to the evening of the 28th, when they died away, and have not since been renewed.

On former occasions I have brought to your Lordship's notice the valuable services performed during this campaign by the Royal Artillery.

Throughout the Battle of the Aisne they have displayed the same skill, endurance and tenacity, and I deeply appreciate the work they have done.

Sir David Henderson and the Royal Flying Corps under his command have again proved their incalculable value. Great strides have been made in the development of the use of aircraft in the tactical sphere by establishing effective communication between aircraft and units in action.

It is difficult to describe adequately and accurately the great strain to which officers and men were subjected almost every hour of the day and night throughout this battle.

I have described above the severe character of the artillery fire which was directed from morning till night, not only upon the trenches, but over the whole surface of the ground occupied by our Forces. It was not until a few days before the position was evacuated that the heavy guns were removed and the fire slackened. Attack and counter-attack occurred at all hours of the night and day throughout the whole position, demanding extreme vigilance, and permitting only a minimum of rest.

The fact that between the 12th September to the date of this despatch the total numbers of killed, wounded and missing reached the figures amounting to 561 officers, 12,980 men, proves the severity of the struggle.

The tax on the endurance of the troops was further increased by the heavy rain and cold which prevailed for some ten or twelve days of this trying time.

The Battle of the Aisne has once more demonstrated the splendid spirit, gallantry and devotion which animates the officers and men of His Majesty's Forces.

OFFICERS MENTIONED

With reference to the last paragraph of my despatch of September 7th, I append the names of officers, non-commissioned officers and men brought forward for special mention by Army Corps commanders and heads of departments for services rendered from the commencement of the campaign up to the present date.

I entirely agree with these recommendations, and beg to submit them for your Lordship's consideration.

I further wish to bring forward the names of the following officers who have rendered valuable service:—

General Sir Horace Smith-Dorrien and Lieutenant-General Sir Douglas Haig (commanding First and Second Corps respectively) I have already mentioned in the present and former despatches for particularly marked and distinguished service in critical situations.

Since the commencement of the campaign they have carried out all my orders and instructions with the utmost ability.

GENERAL SIR HORACE
SMITH-DORRIEN

LIEUTENANT-GENERAL W. P.
PULTENEY

Lieutenant-General W. P. Pulteney took over the command of the Third Corps just before the commencement of the Battle of the Marne, Throughout the subsequent operations he showed himself to be a most capable commander in the field and has rendered very valuable services.

Major-General E. H. H. Allenby and Major-General H. de la P. Gough have proved themselves to be Cavalry leaders of a high order, and I am deeply indebted to them. The undoubted moral superiority which our Cavalry has obtained over that of the enemy has been due to the skill with which they have turned to the best account the qualities inherent in the splendid troops they command.

In my despatch of 7th September I mentioned the name of Brigadier-General Sir David Henderson and his valuable work in command of the Royal Flying Corps; and I have once more to express my deep appreciation of the help he has since rendered me.

Lieutenant-General Sir Archibald Murray has continued to render me invaluable help as Chief of the Staff; and in his arduous and responsible duties he has been ably assisted by Major-General Henry Wilson, Sub-Chief.

Lieutenant-General Sir Nevil Macready and Lieutenant-General Sir William Robertson have continued to perform excellent service as Adjutant-General and Quartermaster-General respectively.

The Director of Army Signals, Lieutenant-Colonel J. S. Fowler, has materially assisted the operations by the skill and energy which he has displayed in the working of the important department over which he presides.

My Military Secretary, Brigadier-General the Hon. W. Lambton, has performed his arduous and difficult duties with much zeal and great efficiency.

I am anxious also to bring to your Lordship's notice the following names of officers of my Personal Staff, who throughout these arduous operations have shown untiring zeal and energy in the performance of their duties:—

Aides-de-Camp.

Lieutenant-Colonel Stanley Barry.

Lieutenant-Colonel Lord Brooke.

Major Fitzgerald Watt.

Extra *Aide-de-Camp.*

Captain the Hon. F. E. Guest.

Private Secretary.

Lieutenant-Colonel Brindsley Fitzgerald.

Major His Royal Highness Prince Arthur of Connaught, K.G., joined my Staff as *Aide-de-Camp* on the 14th September.

His Royal Highness's intimate knowledge of languages enabled me to employ him with great advantage on confidential missions of some importance, and his services have proved of considerable value.

I cannot close this despatch without informing your Lordship of the valuable services rendered by the Chief of the French Military Mission at my Headquarters, Colonel Victor Huguet, of the French Artillery. He has displayed tact and judgment of a high order in many difficult situations, and has rendered conspicuous service to the Allied cause.

I have the honour to be,
Your Lordship's most obedient Servant,
(Signed) J. D. P. French, Field-Marshal,
Commanding-in-Chief,
The British Army in the Field.

STRETCHER BEARERS AT WORK AFTER THE BATTLE OF THE MARNE

Appendix A

Since Thursday, September 10, the Army has made steady progress in its endeavour to drive back the enemy in co-operation with the French. The country across which it has had to force its way, and will have to continue to do so, is undulating and covered with patches of thick wood. Within the area which faced the British before the advance commenced, right up to Laon, the chief feature of tactical importance is the fact that there are six rivers running right across the direction of advance, at all of which it was possible that the Germans might make a resistance.

These are, in order from the south, the Marne, the Ourcq, the Vesle, the Aisne, the Ailette, and the Oise. The enemy held the line of the Marne, which was crossed by our forces on September 9 as a purely rearguard operation; our passage of the Ourcq, which here runs almost due east and west, was not contested; the Vesle was only lightly held; while the resistance along the Aisne, both against French and British, has been and still is of a determined character.

The course of the operations during 11th, 12th, and 13th has been as follows: On Friday, the 11th, but little opposition was met with by us along any part of our front, and the direction of advance was, for the purpose of co-operating with our Allies, turned slightly to the north-east. The day was spent in pushing

61

forward and in gathering in various hostile detachments, and by nightfall our forces had reached a line to the north of the Ourcq extending from Oulchy-le-Château to Long Pont. On this day there was also a general advance on the part of the French along their whole line, which ended in substantial success, in one portion of the field, Duke Albrecht of Würtemburg's Fourth Army being driven back across the Saulx, and elsewhere the whole of the corps artillery of a German corps being captured. Several German colours also were taken.

It was only on this day that the full extent of the victory gained by the Allies on the 8th was appreciated by them, and the moral effect of this success has been enormous. An order dated the 6th or 7th September, by the Commander of the German 7th Corps, was picked up, in which it was stated that the great object of the war was about to be attained, since the French were going to accept battle, and that upon the result of this battle would depend the issue of the war and the honour of the German armies.

It seems probable that the Germans not only expected to find that the British Army was beyond the power of assuming the offensive for some time, but counted on the French having been driven back on to the line of the Seine; and that, though surprised to find the latter moving forward against them after they had crossed the Marne, they were in no wise deterred from making a great effort.

On Saturday, the 12th, the enemy were found to be occupying a very formidable position opposite to us on the north of the Aisne, At Soissons they held both sides of the river and an entrenched line on the hills to the north. Of eight road bridges and two railway bridges crossing the Aisne within our section of front, seven of the former and both of the latter had been demolished. Working from west to east our Third Army Corps gained some high ground south of the Aisne overlooking the Aisne valley east of Soissons. Here a long-range artillery duel between our guns and those of the French on our left and the enemy's artillery on the hills continued during the greater part of the day, and did not cease until nearly midnight. The enemy had a very large number of heavy howitzers in well-concealed positions. The movement of this army corps was effected in co-operation with that of the French 6th Army on our left, which gained the southern half of the town during the night. The Second Army Corps did not cross the Aisne.

The First Army Corps got over the River Vesle to the south of the Aisne after the crossing had been secured by the First Cavalry Division. It then reached a line south of the Aisne practically without fighting. At Braine the First Cavalry Division met with considerable opposition from infantry and machine guns holding the town and guarding the bridge. With the aid of some of our infantry it gained possession of the town about midday, driving the enemy to the north. Some hundred prisoners were captured round Braine, where the Germans had thrown a large amount of field-gun ammunition into the river, where it was visible under 2 ft. of water. On the right the French reached the line of the river Vesle.

On this day began the action along the Aisne which is not yet finished, and which may be merely of a rear-guard nature on a large scale, or may be the commencement of a battle of a more serious nature. It rained heavily on Saturday afternoon and all through the night, which severely handicapped the transport.

On Sunday, the 13th, an extremely strong resistance was encountered along the whole of our front, which was some 15 miles in length. The action still consisted for the most part of long-range gun fire, that of the Germans being to a great extent from their heavy howitzers, which were firing from cleverly concealed positions. Some of the actual crossings of the Aisne were guarded by strong detachments of infantry with machine guns.

By nightfall portions of all three corps were across the river, the cavalry returning to the south side. By this night or early next morning three pontoon bridges had been built, and our troops also managed to get across the river by means of a bridge carrying the canal over the river, which had not been destroyed.

On our left the French pressed on, but were prevented by artillery fire from building a pontoon bridge at Soissons. A large number of infantry, however, crossed in single file on the top of one girder of the railway bridge which was left standing. During the last three or four days many isolated parties of Germans have been discovered hiding in the numerous woods a long way behind our line.

As a rule they seem glad to surrender, and the condition of some of them may be gathered from the following incident. An officer, who was proceeding along the road in charge of a number of led horses, received information that there were some of the enemy in the neighbourhood. Upon seeing them he gave the order to charge, whereupon three German officers and 106 men surrendered.

Appendix B

General Headquarters,
18th September, 1914.

At the date of the last narrative—on the 14th September—the Germans were making a determined resistance along the River Aisne. The opposition, which it was at first thought might possibly be of a rearguard nature not entailing material delay to our progress, has developed, and has proved to be more serious than was anticipated. The action now being fought by the Germans along their line may, it is true, have been undertaken in order to gain time for some strategic operation or move, and may not be their main stand.

But if this be so, the fighting is naturally on a scale which, as to extent of ground covered and duration of resistance, makes it indistinguishable in its progress from what is known as a "pitched battle," though the enemy certainly showed signs of considerable disorganization during the earlier days of their retirement. Whether it was originally intended by them to defend the position they took up as strenuously as they have done, or whether the delay gained for them during the 12th and 13th by their artillery has enabled them to develop their resistance and to reinforce their line to an extent not originally contemplated, cannot yet be said.

So far as we are concerned the action still being contested is the Battle of the Aisne, for we are fighting just across that river along the whole of our front. To the east and west the struggle is not confined to the valley of that river, though it will probably bear its name. The progress of our operations and of those French Armies nearest to us for the 11th, 15th, 16th, and 17th will now be described.

On Monday, the 14th, those of our troops which had on the previous day crossed the Aisne after driving in the German rearguard on that evening found portions of the enemy's forces in prepared defensive positions on the plateau on the right bank, and could do little more than secure a footing north of the river. This, however, they maintained in spite of two counter-attacks, delivered at dusk and at 10 p.m., in which the fighting was severe.

During the 14th strong reinforcements of our troops were passed to the north bank, the troops crossing by ferry, by pontoon bridges, and by the remains of the permanent bridges. Close co-operation with the French forces was maintained, and the general progress made was good. Although the opposition was vigorous and the state of the roads after the heavy rain made movements slow, one division alone failed to secure the ground it expected to. The 1st Army Corps, after repulsing repeated attacks, captured 600 prisoners and 12 guns; the cavalry also took a number of prisoners. Many of the Germans taken belong to Reserve and *Landwehr* formations, which fact appears to indicate that the enemy is compelled to draw on the older classes of soldiers to fill the gaps in his ranks.

There was heavy rain throughout the night of the 14th and 15th, and during the 15th September the situation of the British forces underwent no essential change, but it became more and more evident that the defensive preparations made by the enemy were more extensive than was at first apparent. In order to counterbalance these, measures were taken by us to economize troops and to secure protection from the hostile artillery fire, which was very fierce, and our men continued to improve their own entrenchments.

The Germans bombarded our lines nearly all day, using heavy guns, brought no doubt from before Maubeuge, as well as those with the corps. All their counter-attacks, however, failed, although in some places they were repeated six times; one made on the 4th Guards Brigade was repulsed with heavy slaughter. An attempt to advance slightly made by part of our line was unsuccessful as regards gain in ground, but led to withdrawal of part of the enemy's infantry and artillery. Further counterattacks made during the night were beaten off. Rain came on towards evening and continued intermittently until 9 a.m. on the 16th. Besides adding to the discomfort of the soldiers holding open trenches in the firing line, the wet weather to some extent hampered the motor transport service, which was also hindered by the broken bridges.

On Wednesday, the 16th, there was little change in the situation opposite the British. The efforts made by the enemy were less active than on the previous day, though their bombardment continued throughout the morning and evening. Our artillery fire drove the defenders off one of the salients of their position, but they returned in the evening. Forty prisoners were taken by the 3rd Division.

On Thursday, the 17th, the situation still remained unchanged in its essentials. The German heavy artillery fire was more active than on the previous day. The only infantry attacks made by the enemy were on the extreme right of our position and, as had happened before, were repulsed with heavy loss, chiefly on this occasion by our field artillery.

In order to convey some idea of the nature of the fighting it may be said that along the greater part of our front the Germans have been driven back from the forward slopes on the north of the river. Their infantry are holding strong lines of trenches amongst and along the edges of the numerous woods which crown these slopes. These trenches are elaborately constructed and cleverly concealed. In many places there are wire entanglements and lengths of rabbit fencing both in the woods and in the open, carefully aligned so that they can be swept by rifle fire and machine guns, which are invisible from our side of the valley. The ground in front of the infantry trenches is also as a rule under cross fire from field artillery placed on neighbouring features and under high-angle fire from pieces placed well back behind woods on top of the *plateau.*

A feature of this action, as of the previous fights, is the use made by the enemy of their numerous heavy howitzers, with which they are able to direct a long-range fire all over the valley and right across it. Upon these they evidently place great reliance. Where our men are holding the forward edges of the high ground on the north side they are now strongly entrenched. They are well fed, and in spite of the wet weather of the past week are cheerful and confident. The bombardment by both sides has been very heavy, and on Sunday, Monday, and Tuesday was practically continuous.

Nevertheless, in spite of the general din caused by the reports of the immense number of heavy guns in action along our front on Wednesday, the arrival of a French force acting against the German right flank was at once announced on the east of our front some miles away by the continuous roar of their quick-firing artillery with which their attack was opened. So far as the British are concerned the greater part of this week has been passed in bombardment, in gaining ground by degrees, and in beating back severe counter-attacks with heavy slaughter. Our casualties have been severe, but it is probable that those of the enemy are heavier. The rain has caused a great drop in temperature and there is more than a distinct feeling of autumn in the air, especially in the early mornings.

On our right and left the French have been fighting fiercely and have also been gradually gaining ground. One village has already during this battle been captured and recaptured twice by each side, and at the time of writing remains in the hands of the Germans. The fighting has been at close quarters and of the most desperate nature, and the streets of the village are filled with the dead of both sides. As an example of the spirit which is inspiring our Allies the following translation of the *Ordre du Jour* published on September 9 after the Battle of Montmirail by the Commander of the French 5th Army is given:

Soldiers!

Upon the memorable fields of Montmirail, of Vauchamps, or Champaubert, which a century ago witnessed the victories of our ancestors over Blücher's Prussians, your vigorous offensive has triumphed over the resistance of the Germans. Held on his flanks, his centre broken, the enemy is now retreating towards East and North by forced marches. The most renowned army corps of Old Prussia, the contingents of Westphalia, of Hanover, or Brandenburg, have retired in haste before you.

This first success is no more than a prelude. The enemy is shaken, but not yet decisively beaten.

You have still to undergo severe hardships, to make long marches, to fight hard battles.

May the image of our country, soiled by barbarians, always remain before your eyes. Never was it more necessary to sacrifice all for her.

Saluting the heroes who have fallen in the fighting of the last few days, my thoughts turn towards you—the victors in the next battle.

Forward, soldiers, for France!

> Montmirail, 9th September, 1914.
> General Commanding the 5th Army,
> Franchet d'Esperey.

The Germans are a formidable enemy. Well trained, long prepared, and brave, their soldiers are carrying on the contest with skill and valour. Nevertheless they are fighting to win anyhow, regardless of all the rules of fair play, and there is evidence that they do not hesitate at anything in order to gain victory. A large number of the tales of their misbehaviour are exaggerations, and some of the stringent precautions they have taken to guard themselves against the inhabitants of the areas traversed are possibly justifiable measures of war. But at the same time it has been definitely established that they have committed atrocities on many occasions and they have been guilty of brutal conduct.

So many letters and statements of our own wounded soldiers

have been published in our newspapers that the following epistle from a German soldier of the 74th Infantry Regiment (10th Corps) to his wife may also be of interest:

My dear Wife,

I have just been living through days that defy imagination. I should never have thought that men could stand it. Not a second has passed but my life has been in danger, and yet not a hair of my head has been hurt. It was horrible, it was ghastly. But I have been saved for you and for our happiness and I take heart again, although I am still terribly unnerved. God grant that I may see you again soon and that this horror may soon be over. None of us can do any more, human strength is at an end.

I will try to tell you about it:

On the 5th September the enemy were reported to be taking up a position near St. Prix (N.E. of Paris). The 10th Corps, which had made an astonishingly rapid advance, of course attacked on the Sunday.

Steep slopes led up to heights which were held in considerable force. With our weak detachments of the 74th and 91st Regiments we reached the crest and came under a terrible artillery fire that mowed us down. However, we entered St. Prix. Hardly had we done so than we were met with shell fire and a violent fusillade from the enemy's infantry. Our Colonel was badly wounded—he is the third we have had. Fourteen men were killed round me. . . . We got away in a lull without being hit.

The 7th, 8th, and 9th of September we were constantly under shell and shrapnel fire and suffered terrible losses. I was in a house which was hit several times. The fear of a death of agony which is in every man's heart, and naturally so, is a terrible feeling.

How often I thought of you, my darling, and what I suffered in that terrifying battle which extended along a front of many miles near Montmirail, you cannot possibly imagine. Our heavy artillery was being used for the siege of

Maubeuge; we wanted it badly, as the enemy had theirs in force and kept up a furious bombardment. For four days I was under artillery fire. It is like Hell, but a thousand times worse. On the night of the 9th the order was given to retreat, as it would have been madness to attempt to hold our position with our few men, and we should have risked a terrible defeat the next day. The First and Third Armies had not been able to attack with us, as we had advanced too rapidly.

Our *moral* was absolutely broken.

In spite of unheard-of sacrifices we had achieved nothing. I cannot understand how our Army, after fighting three great battles and being terribly weakened, was sent against a position which the enemy had prepared for three weeks; but naturally I know nothing of the intentions of our Chiefs. . . . They say nothing has been lost. In a word, we retired towards Cormontreuil and Reims by forced marches by day and night. We hear that three armies are going to get into line, entrench, rest, and then start afresh our victorious march on Paris. It was not a defeat, but only a strategic retreat. I have confidence in our Chiefs that everything will be successful. Our first battalion, which has fought with unparalleled bravery, is reduced from 1,200 to 194 men. These numbers speak for themselves. . . .

Amongst minor happenings of interest is the following: During a counter-attack by the German 53rd Regiment on portions of the Northampton and Queen's Regiments on Thursday, the 17th, a force of some 400 of the enemy were allowed to approach right up to the trench, occupied by a platoon of the former regiment, owing to the fact that they had held up their hands and made gestures that were interpreted as signs that they wished to surrender. When they were actually on the parapet of the trench held by the Northamptons they opened fire on our men at point-blank range.

Unluckily for the enemy, however, flanking them and only some 400 yards away there happened to be a machine-gun manned by a detachment of the "Queen's." This at once opened fire, cutting a lane through their mass, and they fell back to their own trench with great loss. Shortly afterwards they were driven further back with additional loss by a battalion of the Guards which came up in support.

An incident which occurred some little time ago during our retirement is also worthy of record. On August 28, during the battle fought by the French along the Oise, between La Fère and Guise, one of the French Commanders desired to make an air reconnaissance. It was found, however, that no observers were available. Wishing to help our Allies as much as possible, the British officer attached to this particular French Army volunteered to go up with a pilot to observe. He had never been in an aeroplane, but he made the ascent and produced a valuable reconnaissance report. Incidentally he had a duel in the air at an altitude of 6,000 ft. with the observer of a German Taube monoplane which approached. He fired several shots and drove off the hostile aeroplane. His action was much appreciated by the French.

In view of the many statements being made in the Press as to the use of Zeppelins against us, it is interesting to note that the Royal Flying Corps, who have been out on reconnaissances on every day since their arrival in France, have never seen a Zeppelin, though airships of a non-rigid type have been seen on two occasions. Near the Marne, late one evening, two such were observed over the German forces. Aeroplanes were dispatched against them, but in the darkness our pilots were uncertain of the airships' nationality and did not attack. It was afterwards made clear that they could not have been French.

A week later, an officer reconnoitring to the flank saw an airship over the German forces and opposite the French. It had no distinguishing mark and was assumed to belong to the latter, though it is now known that it also must have been a German craft. The orders of the Royal Flying Corps are to attack Zeppelins at once, and there is some disappointment at the absence of those targets.

The following special order has been issued today to the troops:—

SPECIAL ORDER OF THE DAY.'
BY FIELD-MARSHAL SIR JOHN FRENCH, G.C.B., G.C.V.O.,
K.C.M.G., COMMANDER-IN-CHIEF, BRITISH ARMY IN THE FIELD.

September 17, 914.

Once more I have to express my deep appreciation of the splendid behaviour of officers, non-commissioned officers, and men of the Army under my command throughout the great Battle of the Aisne, which has been in progress since the evening of the 12th inst. The Battle of the Marne, which lasted from the morning of the 6th to the evening of the 10th, had hardly ended in the precipitate flight of the enemy when we were brought face to face with a position of extraordinary strength, carefully entrenched and prepared for defence by an Army and a Staff which are thorough adepts in such work.

Throughout the 13th and 14th that position was most gallantly attacked by the British Forces, and the passage of the Aisne effected. This is the third day the troops have been gallantly holding the position they have gained against the most desperate counter-attacks and a hail of heavy artillery.

I am unable to find adequate words in which to express the admiration I feel for their magnificent conduct.

The French Armies on our right and left are making good progress, and I feel sure that we have only to hold on with tenacity to the ground we have won for a very short time longer, when the Allies will be again in full pursuit of a beaten enemy.

The self-sacrificing devotion and splendid spirit of the British Army in France will carry all before it.

(Signed) J. D. P. French,
Field-Marshal, Commanding-in-Chief,
the British Army in the Field.

Troyon an Engagement in
the Battle of the Aisne

A. Neville Hilditch

Contents

Troyon an Engagement in the Battle of the Aisne

No conflict in history exceeds in magnitude or importance the battle which commenced on the banks of the Aisne on September 13, 1914. The numbers engaged were upwards of two millions. The area involved stretched on September 13 from Verdun to Noyon, a distance of about one hundred and thirty miles, and included Laon and Soissons, Rheims and Compiègne. The immense battle-line lengthened from day to day. On September 28, its western extremity was Peronne. On October 2, gun defied gun from Verdun to Laon, from Laon to Arras. The Battle of the Aisne, which already summarized many engagements that once historians would have dignified, but modem comparisons forbid to be described, as battles in themselves, became itself part of one gigantic conflict which raged from the bounds of England to the confines of Switzerland.

The thunder of the guns reverberated from the cliffs of Dover to the gorges of the Swiss Jura. But of the whole battle-line of the Aisne no section was more strategically important than that occupied by the British. Not one of the separate engagements, of the British or of the French, which together comprised the battle, was more strategically important or more stubbornly contested than that fought in the woods and on the hillsides around Troyon. The struggle opened with a night-attack in the early hours of September 14. How that struggle was won it is our purpose to describe.

Shortly after midnight on September 14, the 2nd Infantry

Brigade, billeted in Moulins, began to muster. The conditions, indeed, were favourable to a night-attack. Rain fell at intervals. Heavy mist intensified the darkness. Nevertheless, Brigadier-General Bulfin could not but feel anxiety as to his prospects of success. The force under his command, now mustering without bugle-call or beat of drum, only numbered some 4,000 men. It comprised battalions of the King's Royal Rifles, the Royal Sussex, the Northamptonshire, the Loyal North Lancashire Regiments, and was supported by the 25th Artillery Brigade, which was short of a battery. There was ground for believing, and it was afterwards clearly established, that in the previous week the Germans had carefully selected their position, had taken all ranges, had dug gun-pits and trenches, with the object of making a determined stand here, rather than upon the banks of the Aisne between Œuilly and the Pont-Arcy.

Only a few hours before, on the morning of the 13th, the whole 1st British Division had met with little opposition in crossing the river. But the formidable position to which the enemy had retired, south of the line of the Chemin des Dames, looked down at the wooded slopes around Troyon across a wide valley almost destitute of cover. Some of the oldest local inhabitants could remember that this very spot had been held by the Germans in the campaign of 1871. There was another tradition. Historians asserted that, a short distance away, on the hill above Bourg and Comin, Labienus, the lieutenant of Caesar, had successfully defended Gaul against barbarians attacking from the north. Excavation a few years before had revealed in the huge quarries there, now occupied by modem artillery, a subterranean village containing quantities of Gallic pottery and arms.

The Germans might well be expected to offer considerable resistance. Signs, moreover, were not wanting of the constant watchfulness and activity of both the opposing armies. Desultory firing and the occasional screech of a shell broke the silence at intervals. The Medical Corps were at work bringing in the wounded. Great search-lights swept ceaselessly the death-ridden valley of the Aisne. If those great shafts of light, which the mist

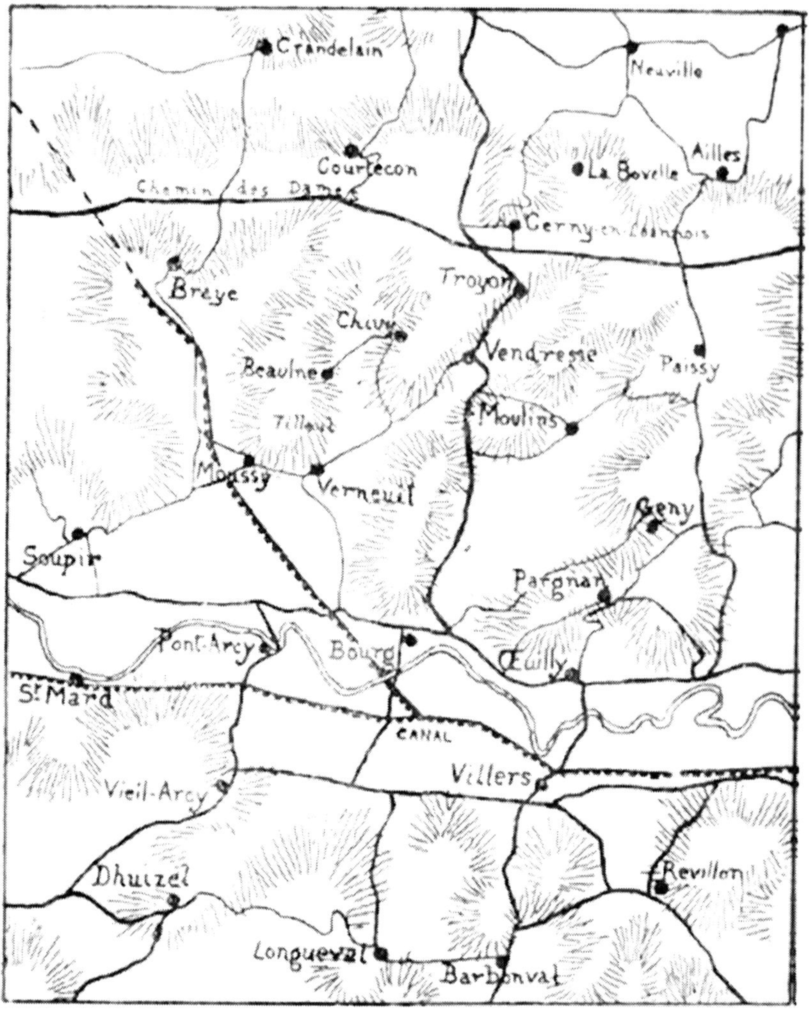

Crandelain
Neuville
Courtecon
Ailles
La Bovelle
Chemin des Dames
Cerny en Laonnois
Breye
Troyon
Chivy
Vendresse
Paissy
Beaulne
Moulins
Tilleul
Moussy
Verneuil
Geny
Soupir
Pargnan
Pont-Arcy
Bourg
Œuilly
St. Mard
CANAL
Villers
Vieil-Arcy
Dhuizel
Revillon
Longueval
Barbonval

hampered but did not destroy, were to play on the woods and fields of Troyon and Vendresse, the British could scarcely hope to deliver their attack without previous discovery. As Bulfin awaited somewhat anxiously the return of the officers' patrol he had sent out to reconnoitre, perhaps he recalled under what different circumstances he had fought in the highlands of Burma, or gained distinction in the South African campaigns. Shortly before three o'clock the officers returned. They reported to the general a considerable force of the enemy near a factory north of Troyon.

Troyon lies on the Laon road, about half-way between Cerny and Vendresse. Wooded slopes of considerable height separate it from where, to its north, near Cerny, the Laon road crosses the Chemin des Dames. West of Troyon, densely wooded country undulates towards the high hills around Braye. East of Troyon a spur of hills rises sharply. Southwards, between Moulins and Troyon, continuous woodland could conceal, but would not facilitate, the approach of the British.

At three o'clock Bulfin ordered the King's Royal Rifles and the Royal Sussex Regiment to move forward from Moulins. The advance was made as noiselessly as possible. Everything depended upon the enemy being surprised. At length the British drew near. The apprehensions of some of the officers were at one point alarmed by hearing a sudden sharp cry. A stray shot, an effect of the general desultory firing, had shattered the arm of one of the men. He could not restrain a cry of agony. But next moment the brave fellow seized a piece of turf with his uninjured hand and thrust it between his teeth. He held it in this position till he was able to crawl back through the lines.

Soon the British came into touch with the German outposts. To conceal their approach now was hardly possible, and they pushed on rapidly till they gained the ground to the north of Troyon. A large factory, occupied by an expectant foe, now impeded further advance. The Germans opened fire. The alarm given, the German batteries in the entrenchments near the factory also opened fire. Meanwhile, the British had formed a firing fine, and had begun to creep forward. The skilful use they made of their ground on that day called forth the admiration of the Germans themselves. All efforts to advance, however, were soon checked by the continuous fusillade.

The black heights, the factory silhouetted against the sky, the dark wooded slopes, presented to the British lying under cover a front sparkling with innumerable points of fire, illumined by the flashes and shaken by the thunder of numerous guns. Light rain and soaking mist aggravated the discomforts but lessened the dangers of the men. Reinforcements were at hand. At four o'clock the Northamptonshire Regiment had left Moulins and advanced to occupy the hills east of Troyon. A considerable time passed with the line, thus extended, keeping up a hot fire and advancing where possible. All efforts to dislodge the enemy from the factory proved futile. It was held in considerable force.

The darkness, the mist, the rain-sodden ground, hampered the advance of the artillery. The east was paling. The shadows in the woods were growing grey. Dawn would soon break. It was not unlikely that the Rifles and the Sussex Regiment would be unable to maintain their position when revealed by daylight. About six o'clock, therefore, Bulfin directed the Loyal North Lancashires, who had proceeded from Moulins to Vendresse, to support their comrades at Troyon in a determined effort to make headway. The effort proved unavailing. Shortly afterwards, however, the 1st Infantry Brigade arrived. The Coldstream Guards were hurried to the right, the Grenadier, the Irish, the Scots Guards to the left, of the 2nd Brigade.

These reinforcements soon made themselves felt. The very presence of the Guards, indeed, was of considerable moral value. The glory of innumerable campaigns had made them jealous of a reputation won upon such fields as Malplaquet and Fontenoy, as Talavera and Barrosa, and as Inkerman. No other corps of soldiers existing could show as fine a record as that which numbered among its achievements the capture of Gibraltar and the defence of Hougomont at the crisis of Waterloo. The Coldstreams particularly could recall an old resentment against the

Troyon ravine Chemin des Dames

foes they now faced. Over a hundred years before, in 1793, British and Prussians lay opposite French entrenchments in a forest. They were then allies. 5,000 Austrians had been thrice repulsed with a loss of 1,700 men. The Prussians were asked to undertake the attack.

Their general, who also commanded the British, sent the Coldstreams, only 600 strong, alone to the assault. It was impossible to carry the entrenchments. The regiment was cut up severely. But it could not be dislodged from the wood.

A vigorous attack was now made upon the German lines. The position was rushed at the point of the bayonet. Unsupported by artillery, the British met with a heavy rifle and shell fire before they reached the enemy's trenches. Tremendous hand-to-hand fighting followed. Fourteen years before, stout Boer *burghers*, impervious to fear of the bullet, had fled in terror at the flash of the deadly bayonet. The Germans had so far shown a partiality for artillery duels, for steady advance in packed masses, for the weight of numbers. They were not accustomed to calculate, nor inclined to rely, upon the dash and the *élan*, as the French say, of a charge with the cold steel. Unable to withstand the furious British assault, they abandoned five guns in a hurried retreat; 280 prisoners were taken to the rear by the Sussex Regiment, 47 by the Scots Guards.

The capture of the factory could only be effected after a desperate struggle and with considerable loss. The Loyal North Lancashires lay opposite the position. It presented difficulties, indeed, which might well cause misgivings to the bravest. Every door was sure to be bolted and barred. Death lurked behind every window. But the Loyal North Lancashires could not hesitate while other regiments on their right and left were striking vigorously at the foe. A party of them forced a passage over shattered doors and barricades, over ruined furniture, over the piled corpses of the slain. Some prisoners and several machine guns fell into their hands. The position thus won was held by men of the Loyal North Lancashire Regiment throughout the day.

The morning, which had dawned amid the roar of action,

was cold and windy, and showed the British how formidable was their task. The line to which the Germans had retreated was strong. Concealed artillery strengthened their entrenchments, which covered a long stretch of rising open ground. The fusillade recommenced and continued with renewed violence. At about nine o'clock the screech of shells coming from the British lines announced that at last the British artillery was able to render the infantry effective support.

Our purpose is merely to record the operations which took place in the neighbourhood of Troyon on September 14. But it is necessary to mention the position of the Allies on either flank of the brigades engaged, which belonged to the 1st Division. To the right of the line of the 1st and 2nd Brigades, on the further side of the spur of hills to the east of Troyon, the troops from French Morocco were entrenched in *echelon*. They came, indeed, from a region on which Germany had once cast covetous eyes. She had had, however, when she sent the *Panther* to Agadir, good reason to desire to make dependants, or at least allies, of the Moroccans. For they had proved terrible foes.

On the left of the 1st Division the 2nd Division had been advancing since an early hour towards Ostel and Braye. The 6th Infantry Brigade, the right wing of the 2nd Division, at nine o'clock reached Tilleul. Here its progress was checked by that artillery and rifle fire which had checked effectually the progress of the brigades north of Troyon. A dangerous interval of ground disconnected the firing lines of these two forces. Sir Douglas Haig grasped the importance of covering this interval. It was more than likely that the enemy would choose a point so vulnerable for counter-attack. The 3rd Infantry Brigade was at hand. At six o'clock it had left Bourg, where it had been billeted during the night, and had at ten o'clock reached a point one mile south of Vendresse.

It was immediately ordered to continue the line of the 1st Brigade and to connect with and aid the right of the 2nd Division. This disposition was speedily justified. No sooner had the 3rd Brigade covered the interval, than a heavy shrapnel fire was

Troyon Military Cemetry

opened upon them, and a strong hostile column was found to be advancing.

The commanding officer of the 3rd Brigade, Brigadier-General James Landon, took prompt and decisive action. Two of his battalions made a vigorous counter-attack. A battery of field-guns was rushed into action, and opened fire at short range with deadly effect. The German artillery, hurling a continuous shower of shells during the whole day upon and around Vendresse, could not inflict on the British such slaughter as one deadly hail of shell and bullet could inflict upon the close masses of German infantry. The advancing column, menaced on either flank, hastily recoiled.

Both British and German lines were now strongly held. The fighting during the whole of the morning and till late in the afternoon continued to be of a most desperate character. Both the opposing forces continually delivered attacks and counter-attacks. British and Germans advanced and retired in turn, surging and receding like breakers on a sea-coast. The men in the firing lines took turns in the dangerous duty of watching for advancing enemies, while the rest lay low in the protecting trenches. Artillery boomed continually from the hill-sides. Maxim and rifle fire crackled ceaselessly in the woods and valleys. At times a sonorous unmistakable hum swelled the volume of sound. The aeroplanes, despite rain and wind, were continually upon the alert.

The troops on solid ground watched them circling at dizzy heights amid the flashes of bursting shells, and marvelled at the coolness, the intrepidity, and the skill of those who controlled levers and recorded observations as they hovered, the mark for every hostile gun, in the open sky. No ditch or wall screened the airmen from the most certain and the most horrible of deaths. Only their speed and their good fortune could elude the stray bullet and the flying splinter of shell which would send those delicate mechanisms hurtling to earth. During the course of the struggle a German aeroplane flew at a great height over the British lines. It was well out of reach of fire.

A British machine rose, swept in a wide semicircle around its opponent, and mounted steadily. The German, becoming alive to these movements, made efforts to attack his adversary from above. He swooped suddenly and fired. The British swerved giddily upwards, and gained the same altitude as the German. Those who watched from below that remarkable duel could see the two machines manoeuvring at a great height for the upper place, and could hear distantly the sound of shots. The airmen showed superb nerve. The struggle ranged up and down for some minutes. Then the British seized a sudden advantage of superior height. The machines seemed to close. The German staggered, its pilot struck by a revolver shot. His slow descent to earth left his adversary in possession of the air. The British aeroplane, skimming and humming downwards amid the cheers of thousands, could well claim to have marked a signal instance of that personal ascendancy which Sir John French so emphatically extols, and which seems to offer chances of Great Britain adding the dominion of the air to her world-wide domain of the seas.[1]

Many instances are recorded of the successes and checks of that strenuous day. At one point the enemy were shelled out of their trenches and abandoned two machine guns. Fifty of them surrendered at the call of ten British. At another point a battalion of the Guards, the Camerons, and the Black Watch delivered in turn a fierce assault upon the German lines. It was necessary to traverse about half a mile of open ground. They went off with a cheer. The air was full of the scream of shrapnel and the whistle of bullets. So hot and so concentrated was the fusillade that the British were compelled to retire with severe loss.

Equally unsuccessful but not less heroic was a charge of the Welsh Regiment. That occasion was rendered memorable by the gallantry of the captain who, struck down while leading the charge and laying about him with an empty rifle, kept uttering dying exhortations of 'Stick it, Welsh!' 'Stick it, Welsh!' His men

---

1. It cannot be claimed as certain that this occurrence took place on September 14. Nevertheless, the evidence is sufficiently strong to warrant its insertion in the narrative of that day's events.

The German retreat of the Battle of the Marne

were, indeed, compelled to retire over his body. But such was the devotion he had inspired that his soldier-servant, afterwards rewarded for his courage with the Victoria Cross, ran out about a hundred yards, exposed to heavy fire, to pick up and bring back to cover his mortally wounded captain. The energy and tenacity with which they were assailed, however, prompted some Germans to fall back upon a base expedient.

A white flag was seen to flutter out at one point in the German lines. It was the token of surrender. A body of the Coldstreams, Grenadiers, Irish Guards, and Connaughts[2] went forward to take the prisoners. No sooner were they well in the open than outburst a ring of fire from concealed artillery. The Germans who had affected to surrender poured in a hot rifle fire. The British, caught in a trap, were cut up in face of a withering fusillade. They perished as martyrs to the unsuspecting faith of chivalry, and as victims of the most disgraceful form of treachery.

It was about four o'clock in the afternoon before a perceptible weakening of the German counter-attacks and resistance indicated that a general advance might safely be undertaken. Sir Douglas Haig ordered his whole corps to push forward. The enemy still offered considerable opposition, and maintained very heavy artillery and rifle fire. It was not found possible to advance far. Cerny was in possession of the Germans. The day had been long and strenuous. The enemy had been forced back a considerable distance. The troops were very weary. Nevertheless, most of the contested ground, from the Chemin des Dames on the right to Chivy onwards, was occupied by the British before night fell.

The 1st Army Corps, and particularly the 1st Division of that corps, had, indeed, good reason to be satisfied with the result of the day's operations. They had gained a very considerable stretch of difficult and dangerous ground, covered with woods that harboured the infantry and concealed the artillery of the enemy. They had had to contest every yard, to dig trenches continually,

---

2. *Irish Regiments During the Great War* by Michael MacDonagh also published by Leonaur.

95

to creep forward slowly, and occasionally to retire. They had captured 600 prisoners and twelve guns. They had repulsed repeated and prolonged attacks. The commander-in-chief asserted in a
dispatch that the advanced and commanding position they had
won alone enabled him to maintain his ground for more than
three weeks of very severe fighting on the northern bank of the
Aisne. The casualties had indeed been severe. One brigade alone
had lost three of its four colonels. But the captured trenches
showed that the Germans had suffered far more heavily.

LEONAUR

ALSO FROM LEONAUR
AVAILABLE IN SOFTCOVER OR HARDCOVER WITH DUST JACKET

AFGHANISTAN: THE BELEAGUERED BRIGADE *by G. R. Gleig*—An Account of Sale's Brigade During the First Afghan War.

IN THE RANKS OF THE C. I. V *by Erskine Childers*—With the City Imperial Volunteer Battery (Honourable Artillery Company) in the Second Boer War.

THE BENGAL NATIVE ARMY *by F. G. Cardew*—An Invaluable Reference Resource.

THE 7TH (QUEEN'S OWN) HUSSARS: Volume 4—1688-1914 *by C. R. B. Barrett*—Uniforms, Equipment, Weapons, Traditions, the Services of Notable Officers and Men & the Appendices to All Volumes—Volume 4: 1688-1914.

THE SWORD OF THE CROWN *by Eric W. Sheppard*—A History of the British Army to 1914.

THE 7TH (QUEEN'S OWN) HUSSARS: Volume 3—1818-1914 *by C. R. B. Barrett*—On Campaign During the Canadian Rebellion, the Indian Mutiny, the Sudan, Matabeleland, Mashonaland and the Boer War Volume 3: 1818-1914.

THE KHARTOUM CAMPAIGN *by Bennet Burleigh*—A Special Correspondent's View of the Reconquest of the Sudan by British and Egyptian Forces under Kitchener—1898.

EL PUCHERO *by Richard McSherry*—The Letters of a Surgeon of Volunteers During Scott's Campaign of the American-Mexican War 1847-1848.

RIFLEMAN SAHIB *by E. Maude*—The Recollections of an Officer of the Bombay Rifles During the Southern Mahratta Campaign, Second Sikh War, Persian Campaign and Indian Mutiny.

THE KING'S HUSSAR *by Edwin Mole*—The Recollections of a 14th (King's) Hussar During the Victorian Era.

JOHN COMPANY'S CAVALRYMAN *by William Johnson*—The Experiences of a British Soldier in the Crimea, the Persian Campaign and the Indian Mutiny.

COLENSO & DURNFORD'S ZULU WAR *by Frances E. Colenso & Edward Durnford*—The first and possibly the most important history of the Zulu War.

U. S. DRAGOON *by Samuel E. Chamberlain*—Experiences in the Mexican War 1846-48 and on the South Western Frontier.

LEONAUR

ALSO FROM LEONAUR

AVAILABLE IN SOFTCOVER OR HARDCOVER WITH DUST JACKET

THE 2ND MAORI WAR: 1860-1861 *by Robert Carey*—The Second Maori War, or First Taranaki War, one more bloody instalment of the conflicts between European settlers and the indigenous Maori people.

A JOURNAL OF THE SECOND SIKH WAR *by Daniel A. Sandford*—The Experiences of an Ensign of the 2nd Bengal European Regiment During the Campaign in the Punjab, India, 1848-49.

THE LIGHT INFANTRY OFFICER *by John H. Cooke*—The Experiences of an Officer of the 43rd Light Infantry in America During the War of 1812.

BUSHVELDT CARBINEERS *by George Witton*—The War Against the Boers in South Africa and the 'Breaker' Morant Incident.

LAKE'S CAMPAIGNS IN INDIA *by Hugh Pearse*—The Second Anglo Maratha War, 1803-1807.

BRITAIN IN AFGHANISTAN 1: THE FIRST AFGHAN WAR 1839-42 *by Archibald Forbes*—From invasion to destruction-a British military disaster.

BRITAIN IN AFGHANISTAN 2: THE SECOND AFGHAN WAR 1878-80 *by Archibald Forbes*—This is the history of the Second Afghan War-another episode of British military history typified by savagery, massacre, siege and battles.

UP AMONG THE PANDIES *by Vivian Dering Majendie*—Experiences of a British Officer on Campaign During the Indian Mutiny, 1857-1858.

MUTINY: 1857 *by James Humphries*—Authentic Voices from the Indian Mutiny-First Hand Accounts of Battles, Sieges and Personal Hardships.

BLOW THE BUGLE, DRAW THE SWORD *by W. H. G. Kingston*—The Wars, Campaigns, Regiments and Soldiers of the British & Indian Armies During the Victorian Era, 1839-1898.

WAR BEYOND THE DRAGON PAGODA *by Major J. J. Snodgrass*—A Personal Narrative of the First Anglo-Burmese War 1824 - 1826.

THE HERO OF ALIWAL *by James Humphries*—The Campaigns of Sir Harry Smith in India, 1843-1846, During the Gwalior War & the First Sikh War.

ALL FOR A SHILLING A DAY *by Donald F. Featherstone*—The story of H.M. 16th, the Queen's Lancers During the first Sikh War 1845-1846.

LEONAUR

ALSO FROM LEONAUR
AVAILABLE IN SOFTCOVER OR HARDCOVER WITH DUST JACKET

THE FALL OF THE MOGHUL EMPIRE OF HINDUSTAN *by H. G. Keene*—By the beginning of the nineteenth century, as British and Indian armies under Lake and Wellesley dominated the scene, a little over half a century of conflict brought the Moghul Empire to its knees.

LADY SALE'S AFGHANISTAN *by Florentia Sale*—An Indomitable Victorian Lady's Account of the Retreat from Kabul During the First Afghan War.

THE CAMPAIGN OF MAGENTA AND SOLFERINO 1859 *by Harold Carmichael Wylly*—The Decisive Conflict for the Unification of Italy.

FRENCH'S CAVALRY CAMPAIGN *by J. G. Maydon*—A Special Correspondent's View of British Army Mounted Troops During the Boer War.

CAVALRY AT WATERLOO *by Sir Evelyn Wood*—British Mounted Troops During the Campaign of 1815.

THE SUBALTERN *by George Robert Gleig*—The Experiences of an Officer of the 85th Light Infantry During the Peninsular War.

NAPOLEON AT BAY, 1814 *by F. Loraine Petre*—The Campaigns to the Fall of the First Empire.

NAPOLEON AND THE CAMPAIGN OF 1806 *by Colonel Vachée*—The Napoleonic Method of Organisation and Command to the Battles of Jena & Auerstädt.

THE COMPLETE ADVENTURES IN THE CONNAUGHT RANGERS *by William Grattan*—The 88th Regiment during the Napoleonic Wars by a Serving Officer.

BUGLER AND OFFICER OF THE RIFLES *by William Green & Harry Smith*—With the 95th (Rifles) during the Peninsular & Waterloo Campaigns of the Napoleonic Wars.

NAPOLEONIC WAR STORIES *by Sir Arthur Quiller-Couch*—Tales of soldiers, spies, battles & sieges from the Peninsular & Waterloo campaigns.

CAPTAIN OF THE 95TH (RIFLES) *by Jonathan Leach*—An officer of Wellington's sharpshooters during the Peninsular, South of France and Waterloo campaigns of the Napoleonic wars.

RIFLEMAN COSTELLO *by Edward Costello*—The adventures of a soldier of the 95th (Rifles) in the Peninsular & Waterloo Campaigns of the Napoleonic wars.

LEONAUR

ALSO FROM LEONAUR
AVAILABLE IN SOFTCOVER OR HARDCOVER WITH DUST JACKET

AT THEM WITH THE BAYONET *by Donald F. Featherstone*—The first Anglo-Sikh War 1845-1846.

STEPHEN CRANE'S BATTLES *by Stephen Crane*—Nine Decisive Battles Recounted by the Author of 'The Red Badge of Courage'.

THE GURKHA WAR *by H. T. Prinsep*—The Anglo-Nepalese Conflict in North East India 1814-1816.

FIRE & BLOOD *by G. R. Gleig*—The burning of Washington & the battle of New Orleans, 1814, through the eyes of a young British soldier.

SOUND ADVANCE! *by Joseph Anderson*—Experiences of an officer of HM 50th regiment in Australia, Burma & the Gwalior war.

THE CAMPAIGN OF THE INDUS *by Thomas Holdsworth*—Experiences of a British Officer of the 2nd (Queen's Royal) Regiment in the Campaign to Place Shah Shuja on the Throne of Afghanistan 1838 - 1840.

WITH THE MADRAS EUROPEAN REGIMENT IN BURMA *by John Butler*—The Experiences of an Officer of the Honourable East India Company's Army During the First Anglo-Burmese War 1824 - 1826.

IN ZULULAND WITH THE BRITISH ARMY *by Charles L. Norris-Newman*—The Anglo-Zulu war of 1879 through the first-hand experiences of a special correspondent.

BESIEGED IN LUCKNOW *by Martin Richard Gubbins*—The first Anglo-Sikh War 1845-1846.

A TIGER ON HORSEBACK *by L. March Phillips*—The Experiences of a Trooper & Officer of Rimington's Guides - The Tigers - during the Anglo-Boer war 1899 - 1902.

SEPOYS, SIEGE & STORM *by Charles John Griffiths*—The Experiences of a young officer of H.M.'s 61st Regiment at Ferozepore, Delhi ridge and at the fall of Delhi during the Indian mutiny 1857.

CAMPAIGNING IN ZULULAND *by W. E. Montague*—Experiences on campaign during the Zulu war of 1879 with the 94th Regiment.

THE STORY OF THE GUIDES *by G.J. Younghusband*—The Exploits of the Soldiers of the famous Indian Army Regiment from the northwest frontier 1847 - 1900.

LEONAUR

ALSO FROM LEONAUR
AVAILABLE IN SOFTCOVER OR HARDCOVER WITH DUST JACKET

ZULU:1879 *by D.C.F. Moodie & the Leonaur Editors*—The Anglo-Zulu War of 1879 from contemporary sources: First Hand Accounts, Interviews, Dispatches, Official Documents & Newspaper Reports.

THE RED DRAGOON *by W.J. Adams*—With the 7th Dragoon Guards in the Cape of Good Hope against the Boers & the Kaffir tribes during the 'war of the axe' 1843-48'.

THE RECOLLECTIONS OF SKINNER OF SKINNER'S HORSE *by James Skinner*—James Skinner and his 'Yellow Boys' Irregular cavalry in the wars of India between the British, Mahratta, Rajput, Mogul, Sikh & Pindarree Forces.

A CAVALRY OFFICER DURING THE SEPOY REVOLT *by A. R. D. Mackenzie*—Experiences with the 3rd Bengal Light Cavalry, the Guides and Sikh Irregular Cavalry from the outbreak to Delhi and Lucknow.

A NORFOLK SOLDIER IN THE FIRST SIKH WAR *by J W Baldwin*—Experiences of a private of H.M. 9th Regiment of Foot in the battles for the Punjab, India 1845-6.

TOMMY ATKINS' WAR STORIES: 14 FIRST HAND ACCOUNTS—Fourteen first hand accounts from the ranks of the British Army during Queen Victoria's Empire.

THE WATERLOO LETTERS *by H. T. Siborne*—Accounts of the Battle by British Officers for its Foremost Historian.

NEY: GENERAL OF CAVALRY VOLUME 1—1769-1799 *by Antoine Bulos*—The Early Career of a Marshal of the First Empire.

NEY: MARSHAL OF FRANCE VOLUME 2—1799-1805 *by Antoine Bulos*—The Early Career of a Marshal of the First Empire.

AIDE-DE-CAMP TO NAPOLEON *by Philippe-Paul de Ségur*—For anyone interested in the Napoleonic Wars this book, written by one who was intimate with the strategies and machinations of the Emperor, will be essential reading.

TWILIGHT OF EMPIRE *by Sir Thomas Ussher & Sir George Cockburn*—Two accounts of Napoleon's Journeys in Exile to Elba and St. Helena: Narrative of Events by Sir Thomas Ussher & Napoleon's Last Voyage: Extract of a diary by Sir George Cockburn.

PRIVATE WHEELER *by William Wheeler*—The letters of a soldier of the 51st Light Infantry during the Peninsular War & at Waterloo.

LEONAUR

ALSO FROM LEONAUR
AVAILABLE IN SOFTCOVER OR HARDCOVER WITH DUST JACKET

OFFICERS & GENTLEMEN *by Peter Hawker & William Graham*—Two Accounts of British Officers During the Peninsula War: Officer of Light Dragoons by Peter Hawker & Campaign in Portugal and Spain by William Graham .

THE WALCHEREN EXPEDITION *by Anonymous*—The Experiences of a British Officer of the 81st Regt. During the Campaign in the Low Countries of 1809.

LADIES OF WATERLOO *by Charlotte A. Eaton, Magdalene de Lancey & Juana Smith*—The Experiences of Three Women During the Campaign of 1815: Waterloo Days by Charlotte A. Eaton, A Week at Waterloo by Magdalene de Lancey & Juana's Story by Juana Smith.

JOURNAL OF AN OFFICER IN THE KING'S GERMAN LEGION *by John Frederick Hering*—Recollections of Campaigning During the Napoleonic Wars.

JOURNAL OF AN ARMY SURGEON IN THE PENINSULAR WAR *by Charles Boutflower*—The Recollections of a British Army Medical Man on Campaign During the Napoleonic Wars.

ON CAMPAIGN WITH MOORE AND WELLINGTON *by Anthony Hamilton*—The Experiences of a Soldier of the 43rd Regiment During the Peninsular War.

THE ROAD TO AUSTERLITZ *by R. G. Burton*—Napoleon's Campaign of 1805.

SOLDIERS OF NAPOLEON *by A. J. Doisy De Villargennes & Arthur Chuquet*—The Experiences of the Men of the French First Empire: Under the Eagles by A. J. Doisy De Villargennes & Voices of 1812 by Arthur Chuquet .

INVASION OF FRANCE, 1814 *by F. W. O. Maycock*—The Final Battles of the Napoleonic First Empire.

LEIPZIG—A CONFLICT OF TITANS *by Frederic Shoberl*—A Personal Experience of the 'Battle of the Nations' During the Napoleonic Wars, October 14th-19th, 1813.

SLASHERS *by Charles Cadell*—The Campaigns of the 28th Regiment of Foot During the Napoleonic Wars by a Serving Officer.

BATTLE IMPERIAL *by Charles William Vane*—The Campaigns in Germany & France for the Defeat of Napoleon 1813-1814.

SWIFT & BOLD *by Gibbes Rigaud*—The 60th Rifles During the Peninsula War.

LEONAUR

ALSO FROM LEONAUR
AVAILABLE IN SOFTCOVER OR HARDCOVER WITH DUST JACKET

ADVENTURES OF A YOUNG RIFLEMAN by Johann Christian Maempel—The Experiences of a Saxon in the French & British Armies During the Napoleonic Wars.

THE HUSSAR by Norbert Landsheit & G. R. Gleig—A German Cavalryman in British Service Throughout the Napoleonic Wars.

RECOLLECTIONS OF THE PENINSULA by Moyle Sherer—An Officer of the 34th Regiment of Foot—'The Cumberland Gentlemen'—on Campaign Against Napoleon's French Army in Spain.

MARINE OF REVOLUTION & CONSULATE by Moreau de Jonnès—The Recollections of a French Soldier of the Revolutionary Wars 1791-1804.

GENTLEMEN IN RED by John Dobbs & Robert Knowles—Two Accounts of British Infantry Officers During the Peninsular War Recollections of an Old 52nd Man by John Dobbs An Officer of Fusiliers by Robert Knowles.

CORPORAL BROWN'S CAMPAIGNS IN THE LOW COUNTRIES by Robert Brown—Recollections of a Coldstream Guard in the Early Campaigns Against Revolutionary France 1793-1795.

THE 7TH (QUEENS OWN) HUSSARS: Volume 2—1793-1815 by C. R. B. Barrett—During the Campaigns in the Low Countries & the Peninsula and Waterloo Campaigns of the Napoleonic Wars. Volume 2: 1793-1815.

THE MARENGO CAMPAIGN 1800 by Herbert H. Sargent—The Victory that Completed the Austrian Defeat in Italy.

DONALDSON OF THE 94TH—SCOTS BRIGADE by Joseph Donaldson— The Recollections of a Soldier During the Peninsula & South of France Campaigns of the Napoleonic Wars.

A CONSCRIPT FOR EMPIRE by Philippe as told to Johann Christian Maempel—The Experiences of a Young German Conscript During the Napoleonic Wars.

JOURNAL OF THE CAMPAIGN OF 1815 by Alexander Cavalié Mercer— The Experiences of an Officer of the Royal Horse Artillery During the Waterloo Campaign.

NAPOLEON'S CAMPAIGNS IN POLAND 1806-7 by Robert Wilson—The campaign in Poland from the Russian side of the conflict.

LEONAUR

ALSO FROM LEONAUR
AVAILABLE IN SOFTCOVER OR HARDCOVER WITH DUST JACKET

OMPTEDA OF THE KING'S GERMAN LEGION *by Christian von Ompteda*—A Hanoverian Officer on Campaign Against Napoleon.

LIEUTENANT SIMMONS OF THE 95TH (RIFLES) *by George Simmons*—Recollections of the Peninsula, South of France & Waterloo Campaigns of the Napoleonic Wars.

A HORSEMAN FOR THE EMPEROR *by Jean Baptiste Gazzola*—A Cavalryman of Napoleon's Army on Campaign Throughout the Napoleonic Wars.

SERGEANT LAWRENCE *by William Lawrence*—With the 40th Regt. of Foot in South America, the Peninsular War & at Waterloo.

CAMPAIGNS WITH THE FIELD TRAIN *by Richard D. Henegan*—Experiences of a British Officer During the Peninsula and Waterloo Campaigns of the Napoleonic Wars.

CAVALRY SURGEON *by S. D. Broughton*—On Campaign Against Napoleon in the Peninsula & South of France During the Napoleonic Wars 1812-1814.

MEN OF THE RIFLES *by Thomas Knight, Henry Curling & Jonathan Leach*—The Reminiscences of Thomas Knight of the 95th (Rifles) by Thomas Knight, Henry Curling's Anecdotes by Henry Curling & The Field Services of the Rifle Brigade from its Formation to Waterloo by Jonathan Leach.

THE ULM CAMPAIGN 1805 *by F. N. Maude*—Napoleon and the Defeat of the Austrian Army During the 'War of the Third Coalition'.

SOLDIERING WITH THE 'DIVISION' *by Thomas Garrety*—The Military Experiences of an Infantryman of the 43rd Regiment During the Napoleonic Wars.

SERGEANT MORRIS OF THE 73RD FOOT *by Thomas Morris*—The Experiences of a British Infantryman During the Napoleonic Wars-Including Campaigns in Germany and at Waterloo.

A VOICE FROM WATERLOO *by Edward Cotton*—The Personal Experiences of a British Cavalryman Who Became a Battlefield Guide and Authority on the Campaign of 1815.

NAPOLEON AND HIS MARSHALS *by J. T. Headley*—The Men of the First Empire.

LEONAUR

ALSO FROM LEONAUR
AVAILABLE IN SOFTCOVER OR HARDCOVER WITH DUST JACKET

COLBORNE: A SINGULAR TALENT FOR WAR *by John Colborne*—The Napoleonic Wars Career of One of Wellington's Most Highly Valued Officers in Egypt, Holland, Italy, the Peninsula and at Waterloo.

NAPOLEON'S RUSSIAN CAMPAIGN *by Philippe Henri de Segur*—The Invasion, Battles and Retreat by an Aide-de-Camp on the Emperor's Staff.

WITH THE LIGHT DIVISION *by John H. Cooke*—The Experiences of an Officer of the 43rd Light Infantry in the Peninsula and South of France During the Napoleonic Wars.

WELLINGTON AND THE PYRENEES CAMPAIGN VOLUME I: FROM VITORIA TO THE BIDASSOA *by F. C. Beatson*—The final phase of the campaign in the Iberian Peninsula.

WELLINGTON AND THE INVASION OF FRANCE VOLUME II: THE BIDASSOA TO THE BATTLE OF THE NIVELLE *by F. C. Beatson*—The final phase of the campaign in the Iberian Peninsula.

WELLINGTON AND THE FALL OF FRANCE VOLUME III: THE GAVES AND THE BATTLE OF ORTHEZ *by F. C. Beatson*—The final phase of the campaign in the Iberian Peninsula.

NAPOLEON'S IMPERIAL GUARD: FROM MARENGO TO WATERLOO *by J. T. Headley*—The story of Napoleon's Imperial Guard and the men who commanded them.

BATTLES & SIEGES OF THE PENINSULAR WAR *by W. H. Fitchett*—Corunna, Busaco, Albuera, Ciudad Rodrigo, Badajos, Salamanca, San Sebastian & Others.

SERGEANT GUILLEMARD: THE MAN WHO SHOT NELSON? *by Robert Guillemard*—A Soldier of the Infantry of the French Army of Napoleon on Campaign Throughout Europe.

WITH THE GUARDS ACROSS THE PYRENEES *by Robert Batty*—The Experiences of a British Officer of Wellington's Army During the Battles for the Fall of Napoleonic France, 1813 .

A STAFF OFFICER IN THE PENINSULA *by E. W. Buckham*—An Officer of the British Staff Corps Cavalry During the Peninsula Campaign of the Napoleonic Wars.

THE LEIPZIG CAMPAIGN: 1813—NAPOLEON AND THE "BATTLE OF THE NATIONS" *by F. N. Maude*—Colonel Maude's analysis of Napoleon's campaign of 1813 around Leipzig.

LEONAUR

ALSO FROM LEONAUR
AVAILABLE IN SOFTCOVER OR HARDCOVER WITH DUST JACKET

BUGEAUD: A PACK WITH A BATON by *Thomas Robert Bugeaud*—The Early Campaigns of a Soldier of Napoleon's Army Who Would Become a Marshal of France.

WATERLOO RECOLLECTIONS by *Frederick Llewellyn*—Rare First Hand Accounts, Letters, Reports and Retellings from the Campaign of 1815.

SERGEANT NICOL by *Daniel Nicol*—The Experiences of a Gordon Highlander During the Napoleonic Wars in Egypt, the Peninsula and France.

THE JENA CAMPAIGN: 1806 by *F. N. Maude*—The Twin Battles of Jena & Auerstadt Between Napoleon's French and the Prussian Army.

PRIVATE O'NEIL by *Charles O'Neil*—The recollections of an Irish Rogue of H. M. 28th Regt.—The Slashers—during the Peninsula & Waterloo campaigns of the Napoleonic war.

ROYAL HIGHLANDER by *James Anton*—A soldier of H.M 42nd (Royal) Highlanders during the Peninsular, South of France & Waterloo Campaigns of the Napoleonic Wars.

CAPTAIN BLAZE by *Elzéar Blaze*—Life in Napoleons Army.

LEJEUNE VOLUME 1 by *Louis-François Lejeune*—The Napoleonic Wars through the Experiences of an Officer on Berthier's Staff.

LEJEUNE VOLUME 2 by *Louis-François Lejeune*—The Napoleonic Wars through the Experiences of an Officer on Berthier's Staff.

CAPTAIN COIGNET by *Jean-Roch Coignet*—A Soldier of Napoleon's Imperial Guard from the Italian Campaign to Russia and Waterloo.

FUSILIER COOPER by *John S. Cooper*—Experiences in the 7th (Royal) Fusiliers During the Peninsular Campaign of the Napoleonic Wars and the American Campaign to New Orleans.

FIGHTING NAPOLEON'S EMPIRE by *Joseph Anderson*—The Campaigns of a British Infantryman in Italy, Egypt, the Peninsular & the West Indies During the Napoleonic Wars.

CHASSEUR BARRES by *Jean-Baptiste Barres*—The experiences of a French Infantryman of the Imperial Guard at Austerlitz, Jena, Eylau, Friedland, in the Peninsular, Lutzen, Bautzen, Zinnwald and Hanau during the Napoleonic Wars.

LEONAUR

ALSO FROM LEONAUR
AVAILABLE IN SOFTCOVER OR HARDCOVER WITH DUST JACKET

CAPTAIN COIGNET *by Jean-Roch Coignet*—A Soldier of Napoleon's Imperial Guard from the Italian Campaign to Russia and Waterloo.

HUSSAR ROCCA *by Albert Jean Michel de Rocca*—A French cavalry officer's experiences of the Napoleonic Wars and his views on the Peninsular Campaigns against the Spanish, British And Guerilla Armies.

MARINES TO 95TH (RIFLES) *by Thomas Fernyhough*—The military experiences of Robert Fernyhough during the Napoleonic Wars.

LIGHT BOB *by Robert Blakeney*—The experiences of a young officer in H.M 28th & 36th regiments of the British Infantry during the Peninsular Campaign of the Napoleonic Wars 1804 - 1814.

WITH WELLINGTON'S LIGHT CAVALRY *by William Tomkinson*—The Experiences of an officer of the 16th Light Dragoons in the Peninsular and Waterloo campaigns of the Napoleonic Wars.

SERGEANT BOURGOGNE *by Adrien Bourgogne*—With Napoleon's Imperial Guard in the Russian Campaign and on the Retreat from Moscow 1812 - 13.

SURTEES OF THE 95TH (RIFLES) *by William Surtees*—A Soldier of the 95th (Rifles) in the Peninsular campaign of the Napoleonic Wars.

SWORDS OF HONOUR *by Henry Newbolt & Stanley L. Wood*—The Careers of Six Outstanding Officers from the Napoleonic Wars, the Wars for India and the American Civil War.

ENSIGN BELL IN THE PENINSULAR WAR *by George Bell*—The Experiences of a young British Soldier of the 34th Regiment 'The Cumberland Gentlemen' in the Napoleonic wars.

HUSSAR IN WINTER *by Alexander Gordon*—A British Cavalry Officer during the retreat to Corunna in the Peninsular campaign of the Napoleonic Wars.

THE COMPLEAT RIFLEMAN HARRIS *by Benjamin Harris as told to and transcribed by Captain Henry Curling, 52nd Regt. of Foot*—The adventures of a soldier of the 95th (Rifles) during the Peninsular Campaign of the Napoleonic Wars.

THE ADVENTURES OF A LIGHT DRAGOON *by George Farmer & G.R. Gleig*—A cavalryman during the Peninsular & Waterloo Campaigns, in captivity & at the siege of Bhurtpore, India.

LEONAUR

ALSO FROM LEONAUR
AVAILABLE IN SOFTCOVER OR HARDCOVER WITH DUST JACKET

THE LIFE OF THE REAL BRIGADIER GERARD VOLUME 1—THE YOUNG HUSSAR 1782-1807 *by Jean-Baptiste De Marbot*—A French Cavalryman Of the Napoleonic Wars at Marengo, Austerlitz, Jena, Eylau & Friedland.

THE LIFE OF THE REAL BRIGADIER GERARD VOLUME 2—IMPERIAL AIDE-DE-CAMP 1807-1811 *by Jean-Baptiste De Marbot*—A French Cavalryman of the Napoleonic Wars at Saragossa, Landshut, Eckmuhl, Ratisbon, Aspern-Essling, Wagram, Busaco & Torres Vedras.

THE LIFE OF THE REAL BRIGADIER GERARD VOLUME 3—COLONEL OF CHASSEURS 1811-1815 *by Jean-Baptiste De Marbot*—A French Cavalryman in the retreat from Moscow, Lutzen, Bautzen, Katzbach, Leipzig, Hanau & Waterloo.

THE INDIAN WAR OF 1864 *by Eugene Ware*—The Experiences of a Young Officer of the 7th Iowa Cavalry on the Western Frontier During the Civil War.

THE MARCH OF DESTINY *by Charles E. Young & V. Devinny*—Dangers of the Trail in 1865 by Charles E. Young & The Story of a Pioneer by V. Devinny, two Accounts of Early Emigrants to Colorado.

CROSSING THE PLAINS *by William Audley Maxwell*—A First Hand Narrative of the Early Pioneer Trail to California in 1857.

CHIEF OF SCOUTS *by William F. Drannan*—A Pilot to Emigrant and Government Trains, Across the Plains of the Western Frontier.

THIRTY-ONE YEARS ON THE PLAINS AND IN THE MOUNTAINS *by William F. Drannan*—William Drannan was born to be a pioneer, hunter, trapper and wagon train guide during the momentous days of the Great American West.

THE INDIAN WARS VOLUNTEER *by William Thompson*—Recollections of the Conflict Against the Snakes, Shoshone, Bannocks, Modocs and Other Native Tribes of the American North West.

THE 4TH TENNESSEE CAVALRY *by George B. Guild*—The Services of Smith's Regiment of Confederate Cavalry by One of its Officers.

COLONEL WORTHINGTON'S SHILOH *by T. Worthington*—The Tennessee Campaign, 1862, by an Officer of the Ohio Volunteers.

FOUR YEARS IN THE SADDLE *by W. L. Curry*—The History of the First Regiment Ohio Volunteer Cavalry in the American Civil War.

LEONAUR

ALSO FROM LEONAUR
AVAILABLE IN SOFTCOVER OR HARDCOVER WITH DUST JACKET

LIFE IN THE ARMY OF NORTHERN VIRGINIA by Carlton McCarthy—The Observations of a Confederate Artilleryman of Cutshaw's Battalion During the American Civil War 1861-1865.

HISTORY OF THE CAVALRY OF THE ARMY OF THE POTOMAC by Charles D. Rhodes—Including Pope's Army of Virginia and the Cavalry Operations in West Virginia During the American Civil War.

CAMP-FIRE AND COTTON-FIELD by Thomas W. Knox—A New York Herald Correspondent's View of the American Civil War.

SERGEANT STILLWELL by Leander Stillwell —The Experiences of a Union Army Soldier of the 61st Illinois Infantry During the American Civil War.

STONEWALL'S CANNONEER by Edward A. Moore—Experiences with the Rockbridge Artillery, Confederate Army of Northern Virginia, During the American Civil War.

THE SIXTH CORPS by George Stevens—The Army of the Potomac, Union Army, During the American Civil War.

THE RAILROAD RAIDERS by William Pittenger—An Ohio Volunteers Recollections of the Andrews Raid to Disrupt the Confederate Railroad in Georgia During the American Civil War.

CITIZEN SOLDIER by John Beatty—An Account of the American Civil War by a Union Infantry Officer of Ohio Volunteers Who Became a Brigadier General.

COX: PERSONAL RECOLLECTIONS OF THE CIVIL WAR--VOLUME 1 by Jacob Dolson Cox—West Virginia, Kanawha Valley, Gauley Bridge, Cotton Mountain, South Mountain, Antietam, the Morgan Raid & the East Tennessee Campaign.

COX: PERSONAL RECOLLECTIONS OF THE CIVIL WAR--VOLUME 2 by Jacob Dolson Cox—Siege of Knoxville, East Tennessee, Atlanta Campaign, the Nashville Campaign & the North Carolina Campaign.

KERSHAW'S BRIGADE VOLUME 1 by D. Augustus Dickert—Manassas, Seven Pines, Sharpsburg (Antietam), Fredricksburg, Chancellorsville, Gettysburg, Chickamauga, Chattanooga, Fort Sanders & Bean Station.

KERSHAW'S BRIGADE VOLUME 2 by D. Augustus Dickert—At the wilderness, Cold Harbour, Petersburg, The Shenandoah Valley and Cedar Creek..

LEONAUR

ALSO FROM LEONAUR
AVAILABLE IN SOFTCOVER OR HARDCOVER WITH DUST JACKET

LEONAUR

ALSO FROM LEONAUR
AVAILABLE IN SOFTCOVER OR HARDCOVER WITH DUST JACKET

ESCAPE FROM THE FRENCH *by Edward Boys*—A Young Royal Navy Midshipman's Adventures During the Napoleonic War.

THE VOYAGE OF H.M.S. PANDORA *by Edward Edwards R. N. & George Hamilton, edited by Basil Thomson*—In Pursuit of the Mutineers of the Bounty in the South Seas—1790-1791.

MEDUSA *by J. B. Henry Savigny and Alexander Correard and Charlotte-Adélaïde Dard* —Narrative of a Voyage to Senegal in 1816 & The Sufferings of the Picard Family After the Shipwreck of the Medusa.

THE SEA WAR OF 1812 VOLUME 1 *by A. T. Mahan*—A History of the Maritime Conflict.

THE SEA WAR OF 1812 VOLUME 2 *by A. T. Mahan*—A History of the Maritime Conflict.

WETHERELL OF H. M. S. HUSSAR *by John Wetherell*—The Recollections of an Ordinary Seaman of the Royal Navy During the Napoleonic Wars.

THE NAVAL BRIGADE IN NATAL *by C. R. N. Burne*—With the Guns of H. M. S. Terrible & H. M. S. Tartar during the Boer War 1899-1900.

THE VOYAGE OF H. M. S. BOUNTY *by William Bligh*—The True Story of an 18th Century Voyage of Exploration and Mutiny.

SHIPWRECK! *by William Gilly*—The Royal Navy's Disasters at Sea 1793-1849.

KING'S CUTTERS AND SMUGGLERS: 1700-1855 *by E. Keble Chatterton*—A unique period of maritime history-from the beginning of the eighteenth to the middle of the nineteenth century when British seamen risked all to smuggle valuable goods from wool to tea and spirits from and to the Continent.

CONFEDERATE BLOCKADE RUNNER *by John Wilkinson*—The Personal Recollections of an Officer of the Confederate Navy.

NAVAL BATTLES OF THE NAPOLEONIC WARS *by W. H. Fitchett*—Cape St. Vincent, the Nile, Cadiz, Copenhagen, Trafalgar & Others.

PRISONERS OF THE RED DESERT *by R. S. Gwatkin-Williams*—The Adventures of the Crew of the Tara During the First World War.

U-BOAT WAR 1914-1918 *by James B. Connolly/Karl von Schenk*—Two Contrasting Accounts from Both Sides of the Conflict at Sea D uring the Great War.

LEONAUR

ALSO FROM LEONAUR
AVAILABLE IN SOFTCOVER OR HARDCOVER WITH DUST JACKET

IRON TIMES WITH THE GUARDS *by An O. E. (G. P. A. Fildes)*—The Experiences of an Officer of the Coldstream Guards on the Western Front During the First World War.

THE GREAT WAR IN THE MIDDLE EAST: 1 *by W. T. Massey*—The Desert Campaigns & How Jerusalem Was Won---two classic accounts in one volume.

THE GREAT WAR IN THE MIDDLE EAST: 2 *by W. T. Massey*—Allenby's Final Triumph.

SMITH-DORRIEN *by Horace Smith-Dorrien*—Isandlwhana to the Great War.

1914 *by Sir John French*—The Early Campaigns of the Great War by the British Commander.

GRENADIER *by E. R. M. Fryer*—The Recollections of an Officer of the Grenadier Guards throughout the Great War on the Western Front.

BATTLE, CAPTURE & ESCAPE *by George Pearson*—The Experiences of a Canadian Light Infantryman During the Great War.

DIGGERS AT WAR *by R. Hugh Knyvett & G. P. Cuttriss*—"Over There" With the Australians by R. Hugh Knyvett and Over the Top With the Third Australian Division by G. P. Cuttriss. Accounts of Australians During the Great War in the Middle East, at Gallipoli and on the Western Front.

HEAVY FIGHTING BEFORE US *by George Brenton Laurie*—The Letters of an Officer of the Royal Irish Rifles on the Western Front During the Great War.

THE CAMELIERS *by Oliver Hogue*—A Classic Account of the Australians of the Imperial Camel Corps During the First World War in the Middle East.

RED DUST *by Donald Black*—A Classic Account of Australian Light Horsemen in Palestine During the First World War.

THE LEAN, BROWN MEN *by Angus Buchanan*—Experiences in East Africa During the Great War with the 25th Royal Fusiliers—the Legion of Frontiersmen.

THE NIGERIAN REGIMENT IN EAST AFRICA *by W. D. Downes*—On Campaign During the Great War 1916-1918.

THE 'DIE-HARDS' IN SIBERIA *by John Ward*—With the Middlesex Regiment Against the Bolsheviks 1918-19.

LEONAUR

ALSO FROM LEONAUR
AVAILABLE IN SOFTCOVER OR HARDCOVER WITH DUST JACKET

FARAWAY CAMPAIGN *by F. James*—Experiences of an Indian Army Cavalry Officer in Persia & Russia During the Great War.

REVOLT IN THE DESERT *by T. E. Lawrence*—An account of the experiences of one remarkable British officer's war from his own perspective.

MACHINE-GUN SQUADRON *by A. M. G.*—The 20th Machine Gunners from British Yeomanry Regiments in the Middle East Campaign of the First World War.

A GUNNER'S CRUSADE *by Antony Bluett*—The Campaign in the Desert, Palestine & Syria as Experienced by the Honourable Artillery Company During the Great War .

DESPATCH RIDER *by W. H. L. Watson*—The Experiences of a British Army Motorcycle Despatch Rider During the Opening Battles of the Great War in Europe.

TIGERS ALONG THE TIGRIS *by E. J. Thompson*—The Leicestershire Regiment in Mesopotamia During the First World War.

HEARTS & DRAGONS *by Charles R. M. F. Crutwell*—The 4th Royal Berkshire Regiment in France and Italy During the Great War, 1914-1918.

INFANTRY BRIGADE: 1914 *by John Ward*—The Diary of a Commander of the 15th Infantry Brigade, 5th Division, British Army, During the Retreat from Mons.

DOING OUR 'BIT' *by Ian Hay*—Two Classic Accounts of the Men of Kitchener's 'New Army' During the Great War including *The First 100,000 & All In It.*

AN EYE IN THE STORM *by Arthur Ruhl*—An American War Correspondent's Experiences of the First World War from the Western Front to Gallipoli-and Beyond.

STAND & FALL *by Joe Cassells*—With the Middlesex Regiment Against the Bolsheviks 1918-19.

RIFLEMAN MACGILL'S WAR *by Patrick MacGill*—A Soldier of the London Irish During the Great War in Europe including *The Amateur Army, The Red Horizon & The Great Push.*

WITH THE GUNS *by C. A. Rose & Hugh Dalton*—Two First Hand Accounts of British Gunners at War in Europe During World War 1- Three Years in France with the Guns and With the British Guns in Italy.

THE BUSH WAR DOCTOR *by Robert V. Dolbey*—The Experiences of a British Army Doctor During the East African Campaign of the First World War.

LEONAUR

ALSO FROM LEONAUR
AVAILABLE IN SOFTCOVER OR HARDCOVER WITH DUST JACKET

THE 9TH—THE KING'S (LIVERPOOL REGIMENT) IN THE GREAT WAR 1914 - 1918 *by Enos H. G. Roberts*—Mersey to mud—war and Liverpool men.

THE GAMBARDIER *by Mark Severn*—The experiences of a battery of Heavy artillery on the Western Front during the First World War.

FROM MESSINES TO THIRD YPRES *by Thomas Floyd*—A personal account of the First World War on the Western front by a 2/5th Lancashire Fusilier.

THE IRISH GUARDS IN THE GREAT WAR - VOLUME 1 *by Rudyard Kipling*—Edited and Compiled from Their Diaries and Papers—The First Battalion.

THE IRISH GUARDS IN THE GREAT WAR - VOLUME 1 *by Rudyard Kipling*—Edited and Compiled from Their Diaries and Papers—The Second Battalion.

ARMOURED CARS IN EDEN *by K. Roosevelt*—An American President's son serving in Rolls Royce armoured cars with the British in Mesopatamia & with the American Artillery in France during the First World War.

CHASSEUR OF 1914 *by Marcel Dupont*—Experiences of the twilight of the French Light Cavalry by a young officer during the early battles of the great war in Europe.

TROOP HORSE & TRENCH *by R.A. Lloyd*—The experiences of a British Lifeguardsman of the household cavalry fighting on the western front during the First World War 1914-18.

THE EAST AFRICAN MOUNTED RIFLES *by C.J. Wilson*—Experiences of the campaign in the East African bush during the First World War.

THE LONG PATROL *by George Berrie*—A Novel of Light Horsemen from Gallipoli to the Palestine campaign of the First World War.

THE FIGHTING CAMELIERS *by Frank Reid*—The exploits of the Imperial Camel Corps in the desert and Palestine campaigns of the First World War.

STEEL CHARIOTS IN THE DESERT *by S. C. Rolls*—The first world war experiences of a Rolls Royce armoured car driver with the Duke of Westminster in Libya and in Arabia with T.E. Lawrence.

WITH THE IMPERIAL CAMEL CORPS IN THE GREAT WAR *by Geoffrey Inchbald*—The story of a serving officer with the British 2nd battalion against the Senussi and during the Palestine campaign.

CPSIA information can be obtained at www.ICGtesting.com
Printed in the USA
LVOW11s0253121113

360964LV00001B/48/P

9 780857 065421